The Ramsgat

By Steve Ba

An Introduction to the Author

Many years ago, I decided to write a book because I wanted to share some of my life experiences, many of them funny with family and friends although I had never attempted to write a book before, so I had no idea of how to go about it or even how to get started.

I came up with the idea of writing bullet points whenever I thought of something that happened in the past and did this for several months until I had reached about eighty different occurrences, and then began to put them in some sort of chronological order, and finally after about six months decided I was ready to start.

I still had no idea of what to do, so I wrote several introductions for the book and found myself unhappy with them all, I found them all incredibly boring, they did nothing to raise any interest in even my own mind and I don't know how or why, but I eventually started somewhere around the middle!

It seemed at the time an odd thing to do, but I wrote about a couple of incidents and they appeared on paper as I would have wanted, and because this approach seemed to somehow work, I continued writing, sometimes moving forward in time, and sometimes travelling back to an earlier point, and finally, my first chapter was completed even if it was the middle of the book!

I continued work on this book for several years, sometimes two or three times a week, but often several months would go by without touching a keyboard at all, and I eventually did reach around the halfway point in the book when disaster struck and my computer died. There was a bigger problem than a mere deceased computer, nothing had been backed up.

I did nothing with regard to the book for over a year after because everything was suddenly gone, but one day the urge returned and I began again purely from memory and this time I was not going to lose it all, I took precautions and I printed off each chapter as it was written and saw what I thought was a reasonably interesting book, again gradually coming together.

I got around two thirds of the way through and could see my book being finally completed, the end was in sight and a friend then borrowed my finished article to read, to give me an opinion before I worked out how I would get it published when disaster once again struck, my second computer also died!

This time however I was not worried because at least I had a paper copy of everything or thought I had, but my friend somehow managed to lose that too. I couldn't believe it I really thought that he was playing a joke with me, unfortunately he wasn't, everything was once again nothing at all.

I did nothing more for several years after this second disaster because it became clear to me that hours upon hours of time and effort were lost again, and it was also obvious to me that this book was never, ever going to be written.

However…

From the April of 2017 I decided to try and make it third time lucky and set about writing it one more time, and I knew that this was not the way to write a book but at least if I recorded it all on computer, keep another copy on a memory stick and publish it on Facebook I would be able to retrieve it from somewhere, whatever disaster occurred.

I started the book this time at chapter four and actually wrote the end before finally completing chapter seven, hopefully it has gelled together OK and you will enjoy reading about some of my life experiences as much as I have enjoyed writing them.

In October 2018 I finally finished writing the book and handed it to someone in the hope that I would be able to get it published, and at long last here it is!

Good Morning, Sir!

I left school at sixteen and started working with Barclays Bank as an office junior and was given all of the mundane jobs such as making the tea, sorting the mail, answering the telephone and generally keeping the place tidy, and at that time I had no idea how a 'gaggle' of women could be, because I attended an all-boys school and this was a completely new experience for me.

There were, including myself three members of male staff and three women at the branch and I didn't have much respect for two of the women, they were horrible cows and seemed to take great pleasure in bossing me around whilst at the same time, they would sit on their backsides and pretend to be busy.

I dealt with the situation as best I could, letting most of what they said go in one ear and straight out of the other, and after a while, I settled in and became an accepted member of staff and was soon taught to operate the computer and carried out most of the computer work for around a year, and I was eventually given the necessary training, and progressed to dealing with the public on a face to face basis as a qualified cashier.

It was about the same time that I started on the cashier tills, that I encountered not my first sexual experience, but my first with a complete stranger, it happened on a Saturday night with somebody I met at a local nightclub.

Toward the end of the evening having drunk several beers, I gained a little Dutch courage and approached an attractive girl who was around the same age and asked her to dance.

She accepted and we danced the last few songs together, and as we smooched away on the dance floor, she put her hand into the pocket of her jeans, pulled out something and casually slipped it into my hand and I couldn't believe my luck, she had only handed me a bloody condom!

Shortly after, we collected our coats, promptly left the club and headed straight for the beach and found a secluded spot beneath the sundeck where we fumbled around in the dark, kissing and groping before I then put on the condom as best I could, yanked down her jeans and performed the business.

I was so surprised by my stroke of good fortune that I offered to walk her home and It transpired that she was a holiday maker and down from London for the week, staying with her parents in a lovely hotel called the 'Ivyside' which is no longer there at Westgate-on-Sea.

I must have been stark raving mad, the hotel was a good three miles away and in the wrong direction to where I lived but, despite knowing nothing about her not even her name, I carried out my promise and walked her back to the hotel only to find out that she had lost her door key.

It was at about four in the morning by this time and was just starting to break daylight, there was no sign of life anywhere to be seen, and in a moment of sheer wisdom I asked her to point out her room and she did, and by pure chance there was a cast iron drainpipe right next to her bedroom window.

I didn't want to leave her stranded at this time of the morning in a strange place so, I offered to climb up the drainpipe, through the window, and then make my way downstairs to let her in which was a ridiculous thing to suggest, but before much longer I found myself hanging onto the drainpipe for dear life halfway up the hotel wall when the front door down at the lobby burst open, and a very large big fellow in a black suit came running out and was shouting and swearing at me, demanding to know what I thought I was doing.

I scrambled back down the drainpipe and apologised profusely, I tried to calm him down and explained the situation and he finally, reluctantly accepted my apology and sent me packing with a few choice words before he ordered her straight to her room without disturbing any of the other guests.

I walked home and forgot about the incident until the Monday morning. when I arrived at work as usual and I set about getting my till up and ready for the doors of the bank to open for the public at nine thirty sharp.

I was horrified when the doors opened, I was stuck behind the till and my very first customer of the day was the large man that caught me climbing up the drainpipe at the hotel!

I couldn't escape the situation and could feel my face profusely reddening before I plucked up courage, looked up at him fearing the worst and cleared my throat before I spoke.

"Good morning Sir, did you have a good weekend?" I asked, and thankfully he must have reflected upon the events that occurred on the very early hours of Sunday morning and seen the funny side before he displayed a wry grin.

"Probably not as good as you, young man!" He replied, and nothing more was mentioned, then or later about the hotel incident.

Quite a few incidents occurred during my time at the Westgate branch of the bank, one day I arrived for work to be summoned into the manager's office where I very nervously knocked and entered the room.

I thought that I must have done something wrong and racked my brains trying to think of what it could be, but fortunately everything was fine and there was nothing to worry about, he had received notification from head office advising him that the bank wanted him to send me on a team building exercise because they wanted to broaden my outlook on life.

We discussed the contents of the letter and it transpired that the bank were offering the opportunity for me to spend eight days aboard the tall ship 'The Sir Winston Churchill' and were not only prepared to pay any costs incurred, including travel expenses but it would not affect my annual holiday entitlement and to top it all, I would remain on full pay whilst away, and of course I immediately accepted the offer, and around a month later packed my bags and travelled to Newport, Wales to join the ship.

I bought a train ticket that was paid for by the bank, and with my bag packed headed off for Newport via London to join the ship, and almost immediately upon arrival attended a couple of briefings where everybody was welcomed on board, and we were advised of the plans that had been made for the week.

We were split into three groups which were known as watches, all of the safety procedures were explained in great detail, and then we were given a tour of the ship where we were also shown our accommodation which was going to be our home for the next eight days.

We unpacked, ate our first meal aboard ship, and a few hours later she ship left port and headed out into the Bristol Channel, and once safely out we headed across the estuary and then along the coast towards Land's End and the Scilly Isles.

It seemed to take forever, we continuously tacked to port and then to starboard in an attempt to make headway into what was clearly a very strong current, and two and a half days later we finally made it to Land's End.

The weather back at Newport had been fabulous, but it rapidly deteriorated, and in a matter of only a few hours we found ourselves stuck in the middle of a force eleven storm that was hairy to say the least, and hardly any of us had any experience of what we were caught up in.

That was when I first learned the real meaning of *'team work'* as we battled to pull in the sails and keep everything shipshape as things were getting thrown around everywhere, sails were shredding, water was crashing over the decks, and to top it all the majority of people on board were suffering with seasickness.

Everybody was instructed to wear a safety harness at all times due to the adverse weather conditions, and It felt like another world a million miles away from the office that I was used to, I was now surrounded by real danger, and in a strange way it was actually quite exciting although the conditions were in fact so bad that a huge tanker not too far from us, got into difficulties and sank!

We lost radio contact with the shore, the wind was so severe that it snapped both of the ship's aerials, and the BBC had an urgent news bulletin being played, regularly announcing that radio contact had been lost with the tall ship 'The Winston Churchill' and there were serious concerns for her safety, and for the forty five novice crew members!

All of those earlier plans were thrown into chaos, we were forced to alter course to attempt and reach safety and shelter at St Peter Port, Guernsey, and several hours later we docked there, and to say that there were some relieved people on board would be an understatement!

We were instructed to go ashore, find a telephone box to call home as soon as possible as there were lots of very anxious parents awaiting news and of course no such thing as mobile telephones back then, and we were to return to ship immediately to assist with the clean-up operation.

Most were able to contact home to let their parents know they were safe, but I was unable to get through, I tried several times to no answer, and I later learned that my parents knew nothing of what had been reported on the news about us being missing, they were too busy on the piss enjoying themselves at a local nightclub with me out of the way for eight whole days!

With hindsight, they were probably better off being out and having fun rather than glued to the television waiting for news to come through.

We spent the next couple of nights at Guernsey while the storm gradually passed over us, and as expected had a couple of good drinking sessions at the same time.

The weather finally broke and we had some very pleasant sailing, we sailed to Brittany and docked at a small harbour where we had some time ashore before finally setting sail and heading north past the Channel Isles and across the English Channel to end our trip in Weymouth harbour, and fortunately I still had cash with me as our original plan was to dock at London where my return train ticket was paid for.

I bought a new ticket, boarded the train and headed for London with all manner of things running through my mind and I didn't know it at the time, but I think that this was where the seeds were planted which ended up a few years later with a drastic change of career.

Even back then, there was no way that I could see myself being stuck in an office for the next forty years I had just caught the bug, I made the decision to become a commercial fisherman and earn a living sailing on the ocean waves.

Upon my return after eight days at sea, I was asked to write a detailed account of my experience and was asked if in any way I felt any benefit from it, and so I wrote a detailed account and around three months later was offered promotion of which I accepted, and a couple of weeks after that I was transferred to the Herne Bay branch where I met my first wife to be, Bev.

Lost Property

Another of my experiences whilst working at the Westgate bank, was when I bumped into an old school friend called Dean one afternoon to learn that my old school Chatham House was holding some kind of an award ceremony later during that week and it was taking place at the Winter Gardens at Margate.

The Winter Gardens is a major entertainment complex with several function rooms, stages and bars in addition to the main arena, and the award ceremony was being held on the Thursday evening and I decided to go along to it, although I had no interest whatsoever in what anybody might be awarded and recognised for, but thought it would be a great opportunity to catch up with everyone that had stayed on at school.

I finished work on the day in question, and after changing at home I grabbed a few pints at my local on the way to the Winter Gardens, and upon arrival I was greeted by a few mates, Dean already told them I that was going to be there, so I was expected rather than it being a surprise.

We headed for the hall, found a row of seats close to one of the exits and made ourselves comfortable when a couple of my old teachers came to say hello, and I got the impression that they were both shocked to see me and were somewhat taken aback by the way that I was dressed, because unlike the scruffy appearance from my school days, I wore a shirt and tie, smart trousers, shiny black shoes and a pucka sports jacket that in fact belonged to my dad, I often borrowed it when I went out for the evening.

After an opening welcome speech from the headmaster, the awards and recognitions got under way with applause at the appropriate times, an hour or so passed when we started to get bored and fidgety and made a decision to head for the exit as soon as we could get away with it, which we soon did and exited the building.

Once outside I suggested we go for a few beers, some of the lads had a money with them although most were broke, but I had plenty of cash, after all I was in the real world not at school and was on a salary, and I can't remember if I loaned money to them or footed the bill, but regardless of that we were soon necking pints of beer like it was going out of fashion at the George Hotel in Margate.

Whilst there, it started raining and I mean really raining I had never seen anything like it, the heavens just opened it was absolutely torrential, and for those not familiar with Margate, the George is situated on an ancient dried up river with a hill on both sides, and the road headed straight towards Margate harbour, that rain just would not stop, it rained so heavily and before much longer the water ran down the roads on top of the hills at both side of the pub and started to collect right outside the doors.

Before long it looked like a river it was unbelievable, there was no way that the drains could possibly manage, and by the time that last orders should have been called it was over three feet deep out there we were trapped, there was no way that we could possibly leave the building.

The landlord kept the bar open, the police wouldn't have been able to get anywhere near us unless they had a boat, and so we got more and more pissed as the night unfolded, but eventually the rain stopped, and the water level started to recede and I think that we were finally able to leave the building at about four in the morning, and by that time I was absolutely hammered!

I cannot for the life of me recall leaving the building and certainly had no idea how I managed to get home, all I do know is that I woke up at seven that same morning, freezing cold with wet feet and I had slept in my dad's car although I did not have his jacket with me, I assumed I left it at the George being in the state I was in, and assumed that I had slept in the car rather than wake my parents at stupid o clock in the morning.

Later that morning, I telephoned the pub to enquire about my jacket but to my dismay was told that I definitely had it on when I left the pub and they also told me the direction I had staggered away in so not only was I confused about this, I was very worried, my dad was going to go mad when he found out and to make matters worse, all of the keys to the bank at Westgate were in the pocket, the front door keys, the safe keys and till keys, literally the keys to absolutely everything.

I walked back to the George in every direction that I could have possibly taken checking gardens, looking under hedges and even looking under cars and was by this time becoming very worried, how the hell was I going to explain this at the bank?

I called in sick and spent the rest of the day searching to no avail for those bloody keys, and to say I was worried was a huge understatement I thought that I was going to lose my job, I was so desperate that I found myself looking in ridiculous places including the fridge, but the jacket and keys were nowhere to be found.

I went into work on the Monday morning and advised the manager of the loss of keys and he was of course very concerned and pointed out the seriousness of the situation, I was instructed to immediately contact the police and report the loss.

I sat in a small back office where I could not be overheard and nervously telephoned the police to report the missing bank keys and explained what had happened (or at least what I could recall!) and also gave them a description of the jacket and was asked to hold the line, and was transferred to the lost property department.

The policeman at the lost property department took my very detailed description of the keys that were missing and then of the jacket including the size and make before the phone went quiet, and then after a long pause the policeman spoke again

"I suggest you call in at number thirty five Gloucester Avenue as they have a jacket and keys fitting that description". He informed me, so I thanked him for his help and put down the phone but something didn't make sense, everything I had lost was at a house four doors from where I lived so I notified the branch manager, and he instructed me to go straight there to put an end to this saga, and this I did and couldn't believe my eyes when I got there.

Other than our house, it was the only one with a porch built on the front, I had never noticed it before, but it was absolutely identical to ours and I stepped into the completely wrong porch!

My house keys actually fitted the main door and I entered and hung my coat on the bannister, I must have then realised from the decor that I was in the wrong house and walked back out leaving the jacket behind, and I must have then walked four doors along to the right house and not been able to get in as I had no keys, then of course later woke in my dad's car.

The people at number thirty five were elderly had been woken by the sound of somebody in their hall, and in a state of shock, they immediately called the police who sent a car straight to them, and apparently, two Cops spent the rest of the evening searching for a burglar to arrest.

Fancy that, a bank clerk that burgled houses and left the keys to the bank in his wake!

Not exactly dry cleaning!

There is one other incident that I would like to share before I move on to Herne Bay.

I was advised by my branch manager that the best and only way to gain promotion and further my career with the bank would be to study and gain pass marks in what were recognised banking and financial examinations.

I enrolled at Canterbury College for a couple of subjects, I think one was advanced or applied math and the other was economics. One thing is for sure, both were the most boring topics you could ever have to sit through.

I was given every Wednesday afternoon off from work to carry out my studies at the university, and I suppose this was some kind of consolation for my efforts. I made friends with a couple of guys who worked at the other high street banks, Chris and Phil. They both managed to enroll for the same courses and managed to get the same time off work for their studies.

At first, we were all keen to get on and climb the ladder of success with our respective employers, we were always punctual when attending college and worked hard with any coursework that was given. Unfortunately, it didn't last long we soon got bored with the classroom and within a matter of weeks we ended up travelling to Canterbury as planned but not for college. Drinking and darts seemed a much better idea and we ended up as regulars at a few Canterbury watering holes scattered around the city.

During one particular Wednesday the sun shone and a tour of the pubs seemed a much better option than attending college, so we climbed off the bus when it arrived at the depot and headed for the Coach and Horses public house for a spot of lunch and a few games of pool. I was wearing new clothes at the time that I bought a week earlier. I had a dark dusty pink suit and a maroon shirt with matching tie!

We ate lunch, played a few rounds of pool and then headed off to the next pub, and a pub crawl developed. We visited half a dozen places before returning to the Coach and Horses, and as the afternoon progressed, we started to get hammered and became quite noisy.

A group of lads were in the pub from the army barracks and we ended up having some kind of a pool competition, and I can't remember what the rules were, but they definitely involved drink and by about eight o clock that evening I was as drunk as a skunk!

I couldn't see the problem, but the two guys I was with were getting very concerned as to how they were going to get me back to Margate. We left the pub and they helped me cross the road to the bus station to wait for our bus home, and all we could remember was that it was the number eight and if we missed it there would not be another for an hour.

When the bus arrived, the driver was reluctant to let me get on board but after a few little white lies from the other two, giving the driver some sort of bullshit story about celebrating my birthday did the trick, and he eventually agreed to let me get on.

The journey to Margate took around an hour, and before we had even got out of Canterbury my head was spinning, I felt terrible and broke out in a cold sweat. I tried closing my eyes hoping that it would go away but it just got worse. I knew I was going to throw up but was unable to do anything about it, I didn't even have the ability to get off the bus.

I glanced around to see several people staring at me and then without a word of warning I launched absolutely everywhere!

There was vomit all over the floor, I had reached at least the next four rows in front of me it was dripping off the hand rails, it was all over the seats and even the windows were smothered with it. I just sat there in it, my suit was ruined but that was the least of my worries. My only wish at the time was to curl up and die.

The driver was really pissed, he stopped the bus and demanded that I got off, my mates pleaded with him we were in the middle of nowhere and I couldn't even stand up.

He reluctantly gave in and let me remain on-board for the rest of the journey. It was a fucking nightmare, I had earlier drank several rum and blackcurrants on top of far too much beer, and the blackcurrant could clearly be seen with the colour of my vomit.

When the bus went uphill it was running to the back of the bus and when it went downhill it was running to the front. People were having to lift their feet as it surged past them, many managed to find seats on the opposite side of the bus, but it was all too much for one elderly gentleman he couldn't handle what was going on and also ended up being sick!

The bus eventually made it to Margate Harbour where a very angry driver tried to apologise to all the other passengers and insisted on me giving him my name and address, and advised me that the bus company would send a bill to cover the cost of cleaning everything and obviously, despite the state that I was in, I had the sense to give him a Mickey Mouse name and address to not face that bill.

The lads attempted to get me a taxi home but they had more chance of seeing god walk down Margate high street, several cars pulled up but drove straight off when they saw the state of me, and in the end they had no choice other than to virtually carry me home. I have no idea how long it took but I lived a good two and a half miles from the harbour so it definitely wasn't a ten minute stroll.

When we finally got there, they propped me up against the door and rang the bell and legged it before anyone could answer the door. My brother Russell opened that door, took a bemused look at me and then shouted something.

"Dad I think you had better come here!"

My old man took a good look at me and wasn't amused at all. He ordered me to go around the side of the house and to wait for him in the back garden, there was no way on earth he was going to let me into the house.

I staggered to the back garden and stood there like a complete idiot, and a couple of minutes passed before my dad appeared from the kitchen.

He wanted to know what the bloody hell was going on, I tried to justify myself and as I was doing this he turned the outside tap on and turned the hosepipe on me he fucking drenched me from head to toe and it was freezing, but talk about sobering up quickly, I didn't know what hit me!

He then stripped me off to my underpants and stuck all my clothes into a black sack and finally, grabbed a hold of my arm and frog-marched me off to bed!

What comes around goes around

I was almost eighteen when I transferred from the bank at Westgate to the Herne Bay branch. It was a much bigger place, it was spread over two floors and there were around fifteen to twenty employees.

It was great, along with the promotion came quite a good salary increase and finally, I was not regarded as the office junior. I was trained to work in various departments including the foreign exchange and sometimes in the security department, and whilst at the branch I was being trained to be the machine room supervisor, and it was there that I met Bev.

Not long after meeting, we started dating and before long we had ourselves a small flat at Cliftonville. She was extremely happy with her job and was the managers favourite she could never do anything wrong.

Although life at Herne Bay had started out great for me, within around six months I became disgruntled with the routine. I think the time aboard *'The Winston Churchill'* made me realise that there was a lot more to life than wearing a collar and tie and being stuck in a lousy office.

I soon detested going to work, everything was a drain and I found it impossible to give one hundred percent effort. Bev and I often talked about emigrating to Canada and even got as far as making an appointment and visiting the Canadian Embassy in London to find out more about the opportunities that were available.

At the time, the bank had just taken on an assistant manager who turned out to be a complete idiot. He refused point blank to allow me the time off to attend my Embassy appointment. I was fuming and regardless of his denial took the day off anyway and went to find out about Canada.

The next day he went absolutely mad and I ended up getting a right roasting from both him and the manager, and from that day forward he had it in for me. A couple of weeks later we had a really busy day and didn't sign out of work until 5.26pm although we were usually gone by five. I booked a half hour overtime, we were paid from nine until five and I started every morning at ten minutes to nine, so as far as I was concerned I felt I was fully justified in doing so.

I went into work the next day to find that he had crossed out the overtime and was refusing to pay me the extra. I had a good argument with him fully justifying my reasons for the extra pay, but he was not prepared to budge. He made up some cock and bull story about receiving a memo from head office regarding the banks running costs. He said that he had been instructed to reduce the branches outgoings hence his refusal to pay the overtime. I didn't believe him but there was not a lot I could do about it, I lost the overtime and he had gained a few brownie points with head office.

Monday mornings were always the busiest time in the bank, the only time it was ever busier was if it was a Tuesday morning following a bank holiday. On these occasions it was nothing short of chaos, there were loads of shops, bars and restaurants that were tourist related and around this era it was very popular to holiday at the seaside in the United Kingdom as travelling abroad was still too expensive for most people.

Over a bank holiday weekend businesses throughout the town would take a fortune, the night wallets they placed in the banks safe were busting at the seams, there were always piles of cheques to process and we were supposed to get this all done and be ready to open to the public at nine thirty sharp.

It was after a bank holiday that I caught the train to Herne Bay and was still severely pissed off. Not only did I not want to go to work, I had been robbed of a half hours overtime. I arrived at the station at eight thirty and decided I would get my half hour back. I headed for a local cafe that I knew did a good fry up where I had a breakfast and then made my way to work. I got there around nine twenty five and knocked on the door and it was dopey that opened it, and I could see that he was stressed just by looking at his face. He pointed to his watch before he stuttered.

"You're late, you know we just had a busy weekend in town so what's your excuse?" He asked.

"It's only nine twenty five, I'm just taking back the time you owe me from last week." I replied and he went absolutely insane, I thought that his head was about to explode!

He was shouting and screaming at me, everybody at the branch stopped what they were doing to see what was going on, he was raging and eventually managed to splutter out that I could not do this before I calmly replied.

"What do you mean I can't do this? I just did!"

From that point on, our relationship became so bad that we couldn't even work in the same room. After repeated attempts he finally got his way and managed to get me transferred to another branch I ended up working at the Canterbury branch, and he was so smug about it.

As far as he was concerned he had got rid of me and made it difficult for me at the same time. Canterbury was a harder place to get to than Herne Bay, nut unbeknown to him, my dad worked at Canterbury so was able to give me a lift to and from work. Not only was this quicker and easier than the train, it was a bloody lot cheaper, I found myself at least half an hour better off in the mornings, no bus to catch to the station and no hanging around for the train, it was great!

If anybody likes a happy ending, the best part is to come and I reckon I had the last laugh. Two or three months after achieving his goal and getting me moved, dopey got the sack from his job, it transpired that all the time he was cutting the banks expenses and refusing to pay such things as overtime, he was dipping his hand in the till and helping himself to substantial amounts of cash that were never his to take.

I have not mentioned his name for obvious reasons, but hopefully one day he might get to read this and if he does, I believe that someone who refuses to pay a justified simple half an hours overtime in a bid to look good, and at the same time robs from his employer is a wanker of the highest order.

Dealing With A Serious Incident

I survived at the bank for around four and a half years, finishing my career with them at their Ramsgate branch. During that period I married Bev and we purchased our first home, a typical first time buyers house in Marlborough Road, Margate consisting of two bedrooms upstairs and a tiny back yard, it was an everyday run of the mill terraced house. Despite both of us working for the bank we were unable to obtain a favourable bank mortgage. You needed to be aged twenty one or over and you had to have a minimum of five years employment with them. We fell short on both accounts so ended up at a normal High St Building Society paying the same interest rates as everybody else.

I had a very close friend Trevor, we are still good mates to this day after all those years, and between us we bought an open trailer boat and some fishing nets. We decided that we could go fishing in the early hours of the morning and earn some cash before we actually went to work in our fulltime jobs, and in theory everything was fine but in practice it was not so easy to achieve. We often ended up late for work and on the odd occasion, didn't even bother to go in.

Decision time was upon me, and after serious consideration I decided to jack my job in at the bank and work somewhere else where the timing could be a bit more flexible and there was really nothing to stop me from doing this. The bank had not even been good enough to give me a staff mortgage. I left the bank and started work at a local furniture store in Margate High Street called Cavendish Woodhouse. It was the same company that my dad worked for at Canterbury. I worked at the shop with my uncle Andy who is sadly no longer with us, and before too long my dad was also transferred to Margate. It became a real family affair and as we all pulled our weight and Head Office got the figures that they wanted, we got away with murder. If I was running late Andy would cover for me or if he wanted to nip off to the bookies I would cover for him. My dad was happy running the shop knowing that every aspect of the business was covered.

I was basically in a position where I could be late for work after going fishing with the knowledge that I would not be pulled over the coals for it. In return one of them would just go home early. It worked perfectly for all of us and head office had absolutely no idea what was going on.

One day, I got up at around three thirty in the morning to go fishing. The boat was on the trailer outside and all we had to do was hook it up to Trevor's van when he arrived, and off we went. He turned up at four, we hitched the boat and headed for St Mildred's slipway at Westgate to launch it and go fishing.

Upon arrival, we were confronted by a concrete post that the council recently placed to stop boats from launching there. To say that we were pissed was an understatement, we had to launch the boat as our nets were already at sea and the next slipway was miles away. There was no way that we could leave our gear out any longer, and faced with this dilemma, we tied a rope around the post, hooked it up to the tow bar on the van and then yanked it out of the ground. Fortunately, this was quite easy to do as the council workers that had put it in filled the surrounding hole with tarmac that was still soft.

When the post was out of the ground we put it in the boat and set about launching, and on the way out to our gear we dropped it overboard, technically disposing of any evidence that it had anything to do with us.

It took around an hour and a half to haul our nets. Apart from quite a few shore crabs and a dollop of seaweed we were pleased with our catch, we had several bass, a couple of lobsters and nearly three stones in weight of dover sole.

As soon as everything was on-board, we headed back to the slipway to get the boat back onto the trailer, and then tow it back to my house. Once the boat was back at mine we would run the fish over to the fish merchant at Broadstairs and get cleaned up for work however, on this occasion Trevor ran the fish and I pulled the nets out of the boat as quickly as I could so that the boat could be hosed down.

I had an old rolled up carpet outside the house that we used for the gear, I unrolled it and quickly pulled the nets onto it, I then rolled the carpet back up to keep the place looking tidy and the last thing I did was to sweep the footpath down so to not upset the neighbours.

I then went into the house, ran a bath and cleaned myself up before getting suited and booted, and then headed off for work at the furniture shop. I met up with Trevor at lunchtime and was pleased to be told that not only was there more fish than we estimated, and the price had also gone up. This meant quite a few more pennies for the day.

Later that day, somebody came into the shop looking for me. I was in the warehouse at that time unloading a lorry full of beds that just arrived when Andy came to find me as the guy in the shop stressed that it was urgent and that he needed to speak to me immediately. I went into the shop and this guy advised me that Marlborough road where I lived was taped off by the police. They were stopping anyone from going down the road and that there were rumours flying around that someone had been murdered near my house.

I told my dad and Andy of the situation and left work to investigate, and sure enough when I got to the road it was all taped off and there were police everywhere. I stooped under the tape only to be stopped by a copper from going any further. I explained to him that I lived at number 43 and had some urgent mail I had to collect. He immediately unclipped his radio and called his supervisor. He explained that I was the guy from number 43 and I was asked to wait as the police officer in charge made his way to me.

I became very concerned, something serious had occurred and whatever it was, it looked like my house was somehow involved. The policeman in charge came over and advised me that a body had been dumped outside my front door. I was then escorted to my house by this copper and it was quite clear that he was expecting me to help him with his enquiries. I couldn't work out what was happening, my house was virtually on the pavement and there was no way a body could have been dumped there without anyone seeing at least something.

We walked to the house and I couldn't believe what I saw, I broke out into hysterical laughter. Trevor had been there a little earlier in the day and for a laugh he removed the wellington boots from the boat and stuffed them into one end of the rolled up carpet. It did actually look like a body was covered with carpet and dumped outside my door. A concerned neighbour spotted it and alerted the police who in turn arrived in droves. This was a joke that looked like it was going to end up being a murder enquiry!

Probably the Best Job In The World!

The job with Cavendish Woodhouse was good and there were several benefits attached. The basic wage was nothing to scream and shout about but there was ample opportunity to build it up. This was done by the way of commission earned on sales made. The commission was low, in fact it was only one and a half percent of the sale value and slightly higher if the sale was completed with the use of finance.

The shop had a regular turnover of over ten grand per week back then equating to about a hundred and fifty pounds plus the commission. Once your commission was added to your basic it was a pretty good wage for the late seventies.

 We worked the shop so that the commission was split down the middle between myself and Andy. I would unload the lorries when they made deliveries, and Andy would take care of the customers. At the end of the week we would have a share of the business made.

Andy did not have a car at the time, so I was trained very quickly to measure up and estimate the cost of carpets at houses. It all sounded straight forward but it was actually quite complicated with such things as winding halls stairs and landings. Not only did we have to calculate how much carpet would be needed from a twelve feet wide roll, we also had to make allowances for cuts and other such things like pattern matches etc. We then had to calculate things like underlay, stair fixings, gripper rods and door thresholds. Our reward for this work was an extra quarter percent commission which we usually added to the basic rate and talked the customer into interest free finance. The result was two percent commission on the majority of our carpet sales.

An attractive lady came into the shop and was browsing through our carpet department, she called me over and made enquiries about purchasing a new carpet. I gave her as much information as I could and made an appointment to call around to her house later in the week and measure up the room that needed carpeting.

As per our arrangement, I called at the address that she had given me at seven thirty in the evening. I was a little nervous, apart from a quick bit of training in the shop my carpeting knowledge was to say the least limited, and this was my first ever house call.

I couldn't believe it when this attractive woman opened the door, she was standing in front of me in a virtually transparent negligee. A huge pair of firm boobs with gob-stopper erect nipples staring me straight in the face. To top it all she had the smallest pair of striped knickers that you could ever imagine, and she seemed to be looking at me with a very inviting smile.

"I take it you're to measure up the carpet, it's for my bedroom so I'll take you upstairs and show you the way" She said, and with that she slowly made her way upstairs gently moving her bottom cheeks from side to side.

Nothing was left to the imagination, it was pretty obvious I was going to get laid, and once at the top of the stairs she sauntered across the landing and into the bedroom. I eagerly followed, by now I had got a raging hard on and the last thing on my mind was the bloody carpet. I was thinking to myself that I definitely had one of the best jobs in the world if opportunities like this came along.

How wrong could I have been?

I walked into the bedroom and was totally stunned, there was some hairy man lying in the bed smoking a cigarette. He had a mug of tea on the side and he was reading the newspaper. It turned out that he was her husband, talk about coming down to earth with a bang!

I was dumb-struck. a very attractive woman earlier opened the door, and she may as well have been naked and invited me up to her bedroom. On entering her bedroom I found her husband in the bed and I later discovered was a copper!

I quickly measured up the room for the carpet and made arrangements to phone the next day with the costings. The evening played on my mind for weeks, imagine what I could've have found myself in if I had groped this woman on the stairs. Nobody in my position would have ever imagined that there was a bloke in the bedroom never mind a copper. I could have been charged with all sorts of things had I carried out what was thinking at the time.

The Mad Chef

I lasted a few years at the furniture shop before the sea finally got the better of me. It was like a magnet that kept pulling me and eventually I packed up any form of 'normal' employment to become a fulltime commercial fisherman.

I fished out of Margate Harbour for about a year and then decided to make Broadstairs my base. Broadstairs was a lovely picturesque harbour to work from and we were the only fulltime boat operating out of there. We had the added bonus of getting on with everyone else that worked in the vicinity.

Sid the Harbour Master was particularly helpful. We always made sure that he got a good feed of fish and in return he would put a chalkboard up for the public to see. It would advise people of when we were due in and it would also have written on it what we would probably have on board for sale, it was great.

We sold fish on the harbour which was always paid in cash, we never declared any of it to the taxman and to top it all, the fishermen based at Margate and Ramsgate had no idea what we were catching. By the time we got to our fish merchant over half of our catch would have been sold on the wall. Any fisherman from one of the other harbours that bothered to check our weighing in book automatically assumed we were idiots with no idea of how to catch fish. We were certainly not landing enough to make them want to follow us.

I became friendly with a guy named Paul Ward who owned a restaurant on the quayside. He regularly bought fish from me, sometimes bass and soles and always crabs and lobsters. If I wasn't fishing and the restaurant was closed we would often consume huge quantities of alcohol together whilst putting the world to rights.

His business had been going through a bad patch and no matter what he tried, he was finding it difficult to get customers through the door. Once he got them in it was great, they brought their own alcohol as he didn't have a license and he served them up great fresh food.

The customer couldn't go wrong, the fact that they had purchased their drink at the local off license made for a good cheap night out.

One day, after several drinks he hit on a brainwave to advertise his business and increase his turnover. He invited all the local news reporters, the local radio hosts and even the woman from Southern TV to the restaurant for a free meal. It was to be an official opening night.

Everyone was treated to a glass of bubbly when they arrived, it was cheap Champaign that had been put into expensive bottles, and everybody was shown to their respective tables for the evening.

Paul personally took the orders, making sure that everyone was happy before setting off to the kitchen to get the cooking underway, and after around ten minutes there was loud screaming and shouting coming from the kitchen. A woman was hysterical and to add to the confusion crockery could be heard getting smashed all over the place.

Suddenly, Paul's wife Jill came charging up the stairs and into the seating area in a state of sheer panic. She was screaming help and claimed that Paul was trying to kill her!

With that, she ran out of the door and along the harbour wall with Paul in hot pursuit. He was armed with a machete and shouting at her at the top of his voice, assuring her that he was going to kill her, and asked her how anybody could be as thick as she was. I would think that they could be heard as far away as the High Street.

Jill reached the end of the harbour, doubled back narrowly avoiding him and then ran down the slipway and on to the beach. Some reporters were outside taking notes, some people were making their way over to the beach to try to help Jill, and the lad that did the washing up earlier called and requested immediate help from the police.

Within five minutes the police were on the scene to investigate. Another twenty minutes passed and the returned to the restaurant where they apologised to everybody for what happened. They then went back to work to ensure that all had a great time, and a night to remember.

Within three days, Paul changed the name of the restaurant. The events of a few nights ago made the papers, the local radio and the TV as he hoped. The new name for the restaurant was to be 'The Mad Chef's Bistro'. People came from miles away, there were nurses, doctors, lawyers, accountants, people from every profession you could think of, they all wanted to meet this so called mad chef that chased his wife with a machete in front of customers.

Paul had achieved his ultimate goal, he had put his restaurant on the map and it was one of the most popular eating houses on the south east coast for many years and all this was down to a staged evening.

Well done to Paul.

Crazy times at the Bistro

I had many good times at the Mad Chefs Bistro, the place was always packed with people literally lining up outside waiting for tables to become available. A lot of toffee nosed posh people used to visit the place on a regular basis, they seemed to find the whole experience good fun. Paul frequently shouted and swore at them and the more he did, the more they enjoyed it. It appeared to me that they liked being belittled, I am sure they had never heard the kind of language that Paul used before, he would call them arseholes and in return they would laugh!

I remember going into the Bistro one night with some lobsters and a couple of boxes of fish after a long day at sea. The place was in absolute chaos, it was crammed to capacity and there was no sign of anybody working apart from Paul. He spotted us as we entered, heaved a sigh of relief and dragged us into his office which was at the time a cave halfway down the stairs to the kitchen. He begged me and John, the guy I was working with at the time to work as all of his staff had mutinied and not turned up for the shift. We were exhausted and really did not feel like it but the promise of wages, free alcohol all evening and a steak at the end swung the balance.

John was given the kitchen to run, he was a fisherman and was now expected to cook gourmet steaks! I was to be the head waiter, taking customer orders and corking their wines for them. It was madness, I was still in my fishing gear and stank of fish and serving customers in a bloody restaurant.

During the course of the evening Paul pulled me to one side and asked a favour of me. He explained that someone had earlier taken some turbot out of the freezer and forgotten to put it back, if it wasn't sold that evening he was going to have to throw it away.

I jumped at the challenge, a party of eight people seated at what Paul referred to as 'the Captains Table' had seen me come in earlier with my catch for the day. I grabbed an empty wine glass and sat down to join them helping myself to a glass of their wine. I then went on to spin this most ridiculous story about how I had nearly gone overboard whilst wrestling this huge turbot over the gunnel. It worked, they asked me where it ended up. 'It's downstairs in the kitchen' I replied, waiting for someone to order and eat it. Five out of the eight at the table opted for fresh turbot as a result of my story.

Paul gave me a wink and took the order downstairs to John in the kitchen to cook. Around half hour later their meals appeared. Both myself and Paul served the table and wished them a very enjoyable evening and a pleasant meal.

The party got eagerly stuck into their meals apart from one, she appeared to be having difficulty cutting into her turbot. I went over to her to make sure everything was OK, only to find out that the it was still wrapped in clingfilm!

How embarrassed I was, I spent around fifteen minutes drinking their wine and spinning some tale about catching a turbot that day for them to be served up a ropey old piece that had been kicking around the freezer for god knows how long and was still in clingfilm!

Another occasion that sticks in my mind was in the height of the summer. I was having a few drinks at the Bistro with some fellow fishermen. Paul was busy, frantically running around trying to keep all of his customers happy. It was about eight in the evening and a very well to do couple entered the restaurant. He was wearing a three piece suit and a bow tie and she had a lovely evening dress on with a matching hat. They had booked a table earlier in the week for the evening. Paul looked up their booking, glanced across the restaurant only to find that their table was still occupied by some people who had an earlier booking.

He explained that he was running late and that it wouldn't be too long before their table would be free. He suggested to them that they sat on the steps outside whilst they waited, the well-dressed woman was not amused, she looked down her nose at him.

"I am not sitting on the steps outside, who the hell do you think I am?" She asked, and Paul shrugged his shoulders.

"Well, fuck off then and come back in half an hour." He replied.

I expected the guy to give Paul a slap but he didn't, he took hold of his wife's hand and they just strolled out of the Bistro. Low and behold, half an hour later they returned to see if their table was ready!

The stories about the Bistro are endless, on another occasion we called in for a few beers after being at sea all day. It was in the middle of winter and we sat around a big open fire. By about nine o clock all of his customers had settled their bills and left. The few beers became a few more and we decided to settle down to a game of Battleships. Paul teamed up with his daughter Louise and I teamed up with John. We were all competitive to the point where losing was not an option. Time flies when you are having fun and before we knew, it was eight o clock in the morning. Not only had we not gone home, we were pretty hammered and we had to go straight back to sea!

The funniest story of them all is the one that follows these last few.

High Tide at Broadstairs

The following story has been told by various people over the years and several parts have been added or removed. This is the actual story as best I can remember.

It was in the middle of summer and we were fishing about three miles off the coast. We were leaving our gear overnight and catching a mixture of skate, dover sole and flatfish. We were also being plagued with spotted dogfish and some large tope. A tope is a member of the shark family and they are worthless as none of the fish markets want them.

We left the harbour early in the morning, hauled our nets aboard and set about clearing them. Amongst the catch was a tope, it must have weighed somewhere between 60lb to 70lb and was about five feet long.

Unfortunately, it was dead so there was no point in putting it back. As soon as we cleared the nets we re-shot them and returned to the harbour with our catch to try to shift it before the sun became too hot. We entered the harbour and were greeted by a crowd of people who lined up to buy fresh fish. We sold everything we caught apart from this bloody great tope.

I decided to try to sell it to Paul but he just laughed at me and asked what was he supposed to do with it, and so I suggested he give us a few beers and use it as a tourist attraction, and Paul being Paul agreed.

The kitchen at the Bistro was downstairs, with the window directly onto the pavement. We pushed the huge fish half out of the window with its jaw resting on the pavement for any passers-by to see because the seafront was heaving with holiday makers enjoying the weather. Before long, people were posing with it for photographs and it became a real talking point, it was there for about three hours, we all thought it was hilarious apart from Jill. She had the right hump, the half of it that was still in the kitchen had been oozing blood everywhere, it had run into the batter mix and it was dripping into the garlic butter. To top it all, it stank, and she was screaming and shouting not only at Paul but at us well, and so we eventually removed it to shut her up.

It seemed such a shame, it had been such good fun we didn't want it to end. At the time, British Telecomm were running an advertising campaign using animals such as koala bears and kangaroo's, and the animals were filmed using the telephone.

Next to the Bistro was a pub called the 'Tartar Frigate' and opposite was an old fashioned red telephone box. We decided that the time had come for the tope to start making some telephone calls. We took it over to the phone box and wedged it up against the inside with the receiver wrapped around its head. It was hilarious we were crying with laughter. It did genuinely look like it was using the phone to call someone.

We got a round of drinks from the pub and found ourselves a prime spot to drink them and watch the fun and talk about a crowd puller, news spread very fast that there was a shark in the phone box by the harbour. We lost count of how many people stopped for photographs it must have been in the hundreds.

The fun got even better, a woman came into the Frigate and asked to use the telephone. She dialled 999 and reported the matter to the police. It was unbelievable, they only turned up with their sirens going and blue flashing lights, God knows what they must have been thinking, I don't know if they were expecting to find a shark or were going to look for a raving nutcase.

They climbed out of the squad car and made their way through the crowd of people. They obviously found it as funny as we did because they burst out laughing. One of them got on his radio and made a call and within minutes, another police car arrived. A copper climbed out with a camera and they all took it in turns to have their photo taken, posing as if they were questioning the shark it was madness, as yet another cop car turned up!

If ever there was a good time to commit a robbery in Broadstairs it was then, over half of the police force were at the harbour having their pictures taken outside this phone box. Without a doubt it was one of the funniest things I have ever witnessed.

At the end of the day when the crowds thinned out and the commotion had died down, we removed the tope from the phone box and chucked it in the harbour to get washed away on the next tide.

A few days later, I picked up the local newspaper on my way to the harbour only to find the bloody thing on the front cover. A group of kids had dragged it off the beach, across the road and up onto the cliff top. On the cliff top there is a famous house where Charles Dickens wrote some of his novels. The house was called 'Bleak House' and was surrounded by a low wall with railings on the top and it all around it. These kids had climbed up the railings and impaled it on the top of them.

The newspaper had got hold of a photo of this and their headlines read *'High Tide at Broadstairs'*

An Expensive leg-over!

During the summer we used to fish mainly for skate and dover soles with the occasional bass and lobster thrown in. From mid-September through to the end of March we worked purely on the cod. The summer fishing usually took the form of putting the gear about three miles out to sea and leaving it overnight. The following day we would retrieve our gear, take the fish out and clear the crabs and any weed that we caught in them. We would then stack our nets and shoot them back again for the next day returning to the harbour with just our catch. In the winter whilst working on the cod it was a completely different ball game.

With the cod fishing we would aim to leave the harbour approximately two hours after high tide. We would steam to the fishing ground with the tide running in a northerly direction and then lay our nets from the southern end running to the north. We would then stay with the gear whilst the tide died and then changed direction to run back to the south. Once the gear had been in the water with the tide running towards the south for about an hour we would set about hauling it back in. Whenever possible we would pick out the fish as we pulled the gear aboard and box them up at the back of the boat. This made it easier to work and helped to keep the fish in tip top condition for when it went to the market.

One day, we put the gear out in a different place, someone from Ramsgate had beaten us to our usual spot, so we waited for the tide to do what it needed to and then set about hauling our gear. The nets were absolutely filled with fish, cod were in them from top to bottom and were flapping for as far as the eye could see. There was no way on this earth that we were going to be able to clear the fish out as we went. We decided to pull everything aboard, drag it around the decks as best we could to keep the boat level (at one point we did not think we would get it all in) and then carefully make our way back to Broadstairs.

It was touch and go as to whether we would get there or not, but fortunately it was a flat calm day and we did. When we got to the harbour the tide was still dropping, making it impossible to enter.

The harbour has a slipway pointing out to sea on the outer side of the wall and I decided to tie up alongside it whilst we waited for the tide to come back in.

Things were not too good at home, we were arguing a lot, we had nothing in common since I had left the 'normal' jobs and truth be known we probably got married when we were far too young. As a result of this I had got very friendly to say the least with the mad chef's youngest daughter Louise, and we ended up having an affair. My sex life at home had virtually ceased to exist so I took advantage of every opportunity I had to put this right elsewhere. The boat was tied on the slipway, it did not make any sense to try and clear the gear onto it as I would only have to run it back to the boat before moving it and I knew that Louise was in the Bistro. Bingo, it was leg-over time!

I was feeling great, it felt like Christmas had come earl, life couldn't get any better, I had a boat full of fish and at the same time was getting laid by the Mad Chefs youngest daughter.

Whilst in the midst of wild and rampant sex, the tide continued to drop and the boat went aground. This was not a problem, it was only sand on the seabed and would not cause any damage to the bottom of the boat.

Unfortunately, everything went tits-up and as the tide came up so did the wind. The gentle breeze we earlier had now swung around to the south-east and was gusting up to about a force six. The sea conditions rapidly deteriorated and it became pretty obvious that we were going to be in trouble.

We waited anxiously as the tide came back in and started lapping around the keel. It rose a little more and then the boat started to rock from side to side. Another half hour and we would be afloat (or so we thought) As the tide rose the waves started breaking into the boat, it was a nightmare of the highest order, we were powerless to do anything about it. There was so much fish on board we needed another foot of water to float. In a matter of minutes the boat was full of water. It seemed there was more water in the boat than out!

Several people came over to help, forming a human chain to get everything off the boat. The anchors were taken off the boat followed by the fish boxes and we dragged the nets off with the fish still in them and up onto the harbour itself.

We then wedged a load of empty five gallon drums under the seat and strapped two forty five gallon drums on to the sides of the boat to try to keep it afloat. Eventually she lifted from the seabed and another guy John Nicholls secured a rope to me from his boat and carefully towed me safely into the harbour where we managed to bail out all of the water before going to sort out our catch.

A local diesel mechanic came straight down and stripped the engine and flushed it through to get any salt water from it. The starter motor, alternator and battery were fucked, but fortunately the engine was absolutely fine.

My repair bill came to about four hundred and fifty pounds and cost me three days fishing for this little escapade. In hindsight, we should have cleared the fish whilst alongside the slipway and then we would have floated easier possibly avoiding this scenario. Instead of that, I was more concerned about using my dick. I think it is fair to say that I had had a bloody expensive leg-over!

A very apt name indeed

It was a rare occasion, but one morning we completely missed the tide due to an extremely heavy drinking session the night before at the Mad Chef's. The gear had been aboard the boat for about five days due to the spring tides and we needed to get it back to sea and earn again. We often arrived back at the harbour in darkness, but it was not common practice to actually put to sea at night. The only exception to this was if we were fishing with surface gear for herrings. However, on this occasion we decided to go in the dark and try to make up for missing the morning.

We took advantage of the extra hours, we were ashore to change the oil filters and did some general maintenance work. We even did a few repairs to the nets. Early that evening we left the harbour on the rising tide and made our way out to the fishing grounds some three miles off. The weather was perfect and the sea looked like a sheet of glass, so we steamed out judging our distance by timing ourselves, our usual method was to line up a few landmarks, but we were unable to do this as it was pitch dark.

When our mission was completed, we turned the boat and headed in towards the North Foreland Lighthouse at full throttle. We were making good headway and we were about a third of the way back when we spotted a yellowy looking light flickering in the distance to the north of us. It didn't make any sense, there were no navigation buoys in that area, and there was no consistency to the way it was flashing. Sometimes a long glow then nothing and then perhaps a couple of quick flickers. To the best of our knowledge, at the time the only time you ever saw a yellow flashing light was an indication that a submarine was travelling on the surface as opposed to under water.

We arrived at the conclusion that it must have been Malcolm, a fellow fisherman who was a part timer. The light we could see must have been marking the end of his herring nets. It was a lovely evening and we had plenty of time on our hands so we swung around to the north and headed over to him for a chat.

It was very confusing, even though it was dark the moon and stars were out giving us a clear line of the horizon. We could see this strange light flickering very close to the water, but there was no sign of his boat. We got to within two hundred yards of this strange light and we could still see nothing. All of a sudden, we heard a voice coming from the water.

"Thank god you saw me!" A voice shouted, and he later explained that his yacht hit something in the water and sank, and he thought he was going to die.

We carefully made our way over to the light and we were absolutely stunned at what we found. There was a guy dressed in dark clothing and he was floating around inside a lorry innertube, which was the sum total of his life saving equipment. To top it all, he was clutching a galvanised bucket. He managed to drain some petrol out of his tank and into the bucket before the boat sank, and he set fire to it to try and attract someone's attention.

Fortunately, his actions worked, because we had indeed spotted him. His time on this earth was obviously not due up, because we saved him from an almost certain death. Had we not had a skin-full the night before, would not have been there to do so.

We grabbed his clothing that was wet through and dragged him aboard. It seemed like he was suffering from the early stages of hypothermia, prompting us to make our way to the harbour as quickly as we could.

Once in the harbour and tied up, we took him to the Mad Chef's where Paul found him some dry clothes to put on and lit the open fire. He had a few drinks and some hot food whilst re-living his nightmare and then we took him to a Shipwrecked Mariner's home in Margate to spend the night.

The moral of the story is that you can live up to your reputation, but it is not always advisable to live up to your name.

His name was Eric Seabury!

An Educational Outing!

The fishing had been quite good and John decided to buy a bigger boat. He located one at Clacton-on-Sea and having had a few sea trials decided to buy it. For some unknown reason it had been named the 'Come Quickly' which seemed a bit bizarre as it was probably the slowest fishing boat to ever operate out of Thanet. Within a matter of days the other fishermen changed her name when calling us up on the radio, we became the 'Premature Ejaculation.

One day, we arrived at the boat at about 4.30am. The tide had just started to drop so we parked the van up, went aboard and carried out all the routine checks such as the oil and water and then set to sea at about ten to five, the plan was to haul our gear, clear the nets, reshoot them and get back to the harbour with our catch by about two o clock that afternoon.

It was a cracking day, the sun was shining and there was nothing more than a gentle breeze blowing. Everything went to plan with a decent catch consisting of quite a variety of fish. We had achieved our goal and our nets were back in the water well within our time schedule. On the way back to the harbour we set about washing, gutting and boxing our catch.

It was in the summer and amongst our catch was around three boxes of smooth hounds (a type of dogfish) that had very little market value. We decided to skin them in the hope of shifting them on the harbour or selling them to a local chip shop for a better price where they would be sold to the holiday makers as rig or rock salmon.

We arrived back at the harbour and then after a wait of around half an hour the tide managed to get into the landing stage. During our wait outside the harbour, we finished skinning the dogfish. This attracted literally hundreds of seagulls to feed on the guts and skins. Being just outside the harbour we were in full view of everyone on the beach. We had attracted the attention of loads of holiday makers who started making their way to the landing stage to see what we had caught. As we unloaded our catch we could hear the click of camera's everywhere, people from inland obviously wanted to show their friends when they returned home from their holiday.

Eventually the crowd thinned out enabling us to get everything up the steps and stacked up ready to sell when a large minibus turned up and parked on the harbour.

The back doors opened and a crowd of girls in school uniform (they were from the Ursuline Convent) got out and stood in line. Two sisters climbed out from the front seats, gave some kind of instructions to the girls and handed them a clip board each, it was obviously some kind of an educational outing that they were on.

Four or five of the girls made their way over to us and politely started asking questions. 'Hello Sir' said one girl 'Do you mind me asking how long you have been to sea today?'

I replied and then another asked me 'What is the name of your boat Sir?' I told her the boat was named the 'Come Quickly'. They were all taking notes on their clip boards. 'What sort of fish have you caught' came a voice from another one of them. I advised them that there were all sorts of fish, some cod, dabs, plaice, dover soles, dogfish, bass, a few crabs and two lobsters. Everything I said was being frantically written down. One of the girls pointed to a box of the skinned dogfish and asked me 'What are those funny looking ones in that box?'

Before I could answer the question, John decided to join the conversation. He picked one up to show them, he waved it about in the air and I don't know how he did it, but he managed to keep a straight face told them that it was a sharks penis. I had to look away, I lost control of myself. These innocent convent educated schoolgirls were only writing it down on their notepads! They asked a few more questions, thanked us for our time and walked off towards the beach.

To this day, I have often wondered what the nun's responses would have been like when they got to reading the school girls reports on their day out at Broadstairs.

Unbelievable

One early morning we cast our nets and it Unfortunately took longer than expected and by the time we finished, there was not enough water to get back into Broadstairs harbour.

Faced with an extremely long wait, we radioed Sid the harbour master and advised him that we were going back to Ramsgate and staying overnight rather than hang around for hours. We motored to Ramsgate, called up for permission to enter and on entry found somewhere to berth the boat for the night.

When everything was done, we walked in the direction of the town to get some pies from the local butchers. My brother worked there so I knew that they would be good and they wouldn't be the usual price! We entered the shop, waited to be served by my brother Russell and purchased our goodies. He told me that he needed to speak to me urgently and we arranged to meet up at lunchtime back at the harbour.

He arrived at about half past one and told me he was in trouble with the Police. He had to go to court for a few motoring offences and didn't want to go on his own. There was no way he wanted our dad knowing about it so wanted to know if I would go with him. I happily agreed to go with him, he told me when the hearing was, and I met up with him an hour beforehand. On arrival at the court house he was given a few forms to read and sign and then we were ushered into a waiting room to await his name being called out.

After about two hours, my brother was summoned to see the judge in court room three. An usher escorted him there and I made my way to the public gallery to listen to the trial. He was asked various questions, his name, date of birth, current address etc. The charges were read out to him. I listened in amazement as the police officer read them out and all I kept thinking was that he was in a lot more trouble than he had let on. It was no wonder he didn't want dad with him, he would probably have had a bloody heart attack!

The cops statement went something like this:

'I was patrolling in my police car on the night in question when I saw the accused driving a Ford Capri erratically in the opposite direction. I immediately turned my car around and with my siren sounding and my blue flashers on attempted to pursue him. As I got closer the accused accelerated away. I followed him as he raced towards Ramsgate at speeds of up to sixty miles per hour. I was horrified, he drove straight through a red light. I stayed in hot pursuit and he took a sharp left in a desperate attempt to lose me. I managed to stay on his tail and to my utter disbelief he drove straight through another red light and turned sharply to the right. There were other cars at the traffic lights and it was not safe for me to follow without stopping. For a short period of time I had lost him'.

I sat in the gallery in silence, the judge said a few words and then asked the policeman to continue with his statement. The copper took a breath and then continued.

'When it was safe to turn at the lights I drove off in the direction that the accused had taken. My radio sounded and the police station were advising me that a car had driven straight into the Co-op Funeral Directors window. Sure enough, on arrival at the premises the car that the accused had been driving was the one that had crashed. I got out of the squad car and went over to investigate. It had been abandoned, there was not a driver to be seen anywhere. I called for back-up and began searching the immediate area. I entered a garden that was attached to the funeral parlour and began searching with my torch in hand. At the back of the garden was a greenhouse, I entered it and found the accused crouching behind some plants that were growing in large plant pots. I asked the accused what he was doing there, and he slowly stood up. He looked me in the eye and said 'What does it look like I am doing, I am watering my tomatoes'

I looked around the gallery to see a few members of the public sniggering, I didn't know whether to laugh or cry, my brother was definitely in the shit, but at the same time it was funny. I looked back to the procedures that were going on and it even looked like the judge was trying not to laugh.

The case ended with my brother being found guilty and being sentenced to fourteen days in Canterbury prison. Without doubt he got off lightly and my main concern now was to break the news to mum and dad and to make up some excuse for his boss so that he didn't lose his job. I told them both the same story, that being he had decided to take a last minute holiday.

He was let out of prison after nine days for good behaviour. He went back to work and told his boss that he had missed his job so much he decided to cut his holiday short so as to get back to work!

Celebrities

My Aunt Kay started work at the Mad Chef's bistro and my first thoughts were that she wouldn't be there long. As soon as Paul screamed at a customer or called her a 'fucking silly cow' she would be gone. I was wrong, she loved it and worked there for a couple of years.

One night whilst she was working, Chas and Dave came in for a few drinks and something to eat. For anyone that doesn't know who they are, they were very popular in the eighties and had top twenty hits with songs such as 'Down to Margate' 'Gertcha' 'Mustn't Grumble' and 'Rabbit'

They sat down and Paul went and joined them after they ordered their food. Kay took their order and in between serving, kept asking them to sing a few numbers. They politely declined her requests but she persisted, she was determined to get them singing.

In the end they gave her a definite no, pointing out that it would be impossible to sing without a piano.

"That's not a problem, my dad has got one back at our house." She replied.

To cut a long story short, they agreed that they would sing a few songs if she could get the piano over to the Bistro. I had just come in from sea and before I knew it arrangements had been made for me to go around to the house with a friend in my stinky van to collect the piano.

My grandad had no idea what was going on, he hadn't seen me for weeks and all of a sudden I had turned up out of the blue to take his piano away!

I arrived back at the Bistro with the piano, Paul shoved a table of four (Who were still eating!) into the corner to make some space and between a group of us, we managed to get it inside. Everybody was treated to a good old singalong.

To be honest, I can't remember much of the evening because to say the drinks were flowing would be an absolute understatement. I don't think anyone including Chas and Dave went home before two o clock in the morning.

On another occasion, Judith Chalmers came into the Bistro. She hosted a very popular television program called 'Wish you were here'. Her job was to travel around different British holiday resorts and show off what attractions were there. They were filming Broadstairs at the time, I can't remember if they were actually filming in the Bistro that evening or had finished for the day and were just out for a meal.

She sat down with her film crew and after a short time, they all placed their orders. Judith Chalmers specifically asked for Plaice as it was her favourite dish. Unfortunately, Paul did not have any plaice, I had had several discussions with him in a bid to get him to start selling flounders or at least to get them on the menu. I was catching about a box a day of them and they were virtually worthless.

We had come up with various names for the dish but as of then he had not sold any.

Paul in his wisdom, decided that now was the time to try it. There is nothing like jumping in the deep end!

He had a television celebrity in the restaurant and he was only going to palm her off with a bloody flounder. Her meal was served with some tasty sort of a sauce on it and it was pretty obvious that she was enjoying it.

In fact, she enjoyed it so much she called Paul over when she had finished to complement him on his food. She said something along the lines of 'I have got to say that that was the best plaice I have ever eaten in my life!'

Paul had a grin on his face, he grabbed an empty wine glass from the shelf, sat down with her and helped himself to a glass of her wine. He then whispered to her.

"Can I let you into a little secret?" He asked. She nodded and he went on to tell her.

"That was not Plaice that was Pegwell Bay Halibut, a dish that is exclusive to the Bistro!"

She totally fell for it and for anyone reading this that has ever eaten Pegwell Bay Halibut at the Bistro when it was open, now you know what it really was.

First Impressions

I spent about five years of my life with this wonderful lady. Unfortunately, she was taken from everybody whilst only in her early forties leaving behind a great husband and a young child that has grown up to be a fine young man. I took the time to check with both her husband (John) and her mum (Joan) before any of my memoires were made public and got the thumbs up from both of them to proceed so here goes.

Although I was fishing out of Broadstairs harbour, many of my friends still worked their boats out of Margate. I still socialized with them on a regular basis, catching up on how people were getting on fishing, anywhere new that had been found, any new gear that was on the market etc.

These conversations usually took place in the Ship Inn at Margate, a pub that was situated between the harbour and the Lifeboat House. It was at the time, the busiest pub by far in town and needed five girls behind the bar just to keep up with the demand for drinks.

When it was rammed full, I used to help them out by collecting all the empty glasses and returning them to the bar to be cleaned and used again. As a result of helping out, I ended up actually working there three nights a week collecting glasses, changing barrels and serving behind the bar. It was great, I was the only bloke in the pub apart from Alan the governor who didn't have to pay for his drinks and at the same time I was getting paid!

Over the next few months I dated several of the barmaids that worked there and eventually started dating Teresa who also worked there. We had both been playing the same game, I had made out I wasn't interested in her and she had done the same to me.

Our first date came after an extremely busy Saturday night, the pub had been heaving all evening and between serving customers and collecting glasses we had both consumed a lot of alcohol. Right at the end of the evening and totally out of the blue, Teresa asked me if

I fancied going out for a Chinese meal. I was single at the time, so without hesitation agreed to go with her.

We cleared the pub as quickly as we could, re-stocked the bar, cashed up, and by a quarter to midnight were on our way to the restaurant.

Once at the restaurant, we were shown to our table and ordered yet more drinks while we had a look at the menu. Our conversation seemed a little bit distant, I can only think it was because it was a first date and we were both on our guard.

We decided on what food to eat and Teresa called the waiter over to place our order. I took this opportunity to nip off to the loo. The toilets in this restaurant were upstairs and access to them was via a grand staircase with highly polished bannisters on both sides.

Teresa waited patiently for me to return, about twenty minutes passed and still she waited. The starters arrived at our table and still there was no sign of me. Another ten minutes passed by and Teresa still sat on her own. Reluctantly she ate her starter having no idea whatsoever about what had happened to me. The waiter came over and cleared her plate asking her if everything was OK. She told him that she was fine. The main course turned up and still there was no sign of me.

Somewhat embarrassed and concerned, she turned to the table next to her where a young couple were having a romantic night out together. She explained to the fellow that her boyfriend had gone to the loo about half an hour ago and had not returned. She then asked him if he would go and check that I was alright. The fellow agreed and left the table and made his way upstairs towards the toilets. I don't think anyone could have expected to see what he found when he got there, he was probably expecting to find someone throwing up with his head either in the sink or down the loo but that was not the case.

It would appear that I had gone upstairs to the loo having had far too much to drink. I had then for some strange reason decided that it was time to go to bed. I had taken all of my clothes off, to the point that I was totally naked! I then neatly folded my shirt and trousers and made myself a pillow with them. I laid down and went to sleep on the landing between the ladies and the gent's toilets! People wanting to use the toilets were having to step over my naked body to get to them and to make matters worse, the guy that had kindly agreed to check on me, was told to 'fuck Off' when he woke me up!

The haunted flat

Despite the way our first date went, we got on well together, she was only nineteen and I was a twenty two year old bloke without a care in the world. It was only a matter of weeks and I had moved into her flat at Cliftonville and our relationship flourished. We lived in the flat for about two years and while we were there, it would be fair to say lots of strange and unexplainable things occurred. I have never been one to believe in ghosts, but this place was definitely haunted.

Numerous things happened that were unexplainable, things would get moved around whilst we were out, pictures would come off the wall and end up in the middle of the room, cold winds blowing from nowhere etc. We didn't take that much notice of them, half the time she thought it was me fucking around and the other half of the time I would think it was her.

One morning we lay in bed chatting and the toilet flushed. I jumped out of bed and rushed to the bedroom door. I looked down the hallway in the direction of the loo to see who was in the flat. The toilet door was wide open. The loo was an old fashioned one with a cistern on the wall above your head. Low and behold the toilet was empty, there was not a sign of anyone having just used it. The eerie thing was the fact that it had flushed and to make matters worse the chain that you pulled to flush it was swinging like a pendulum as if someone had just let it go.

Another time I was rigging nets at home, I used to stretch a rope from the toilet door to the bedroom door. It was a run of between forty and fifty feet. I would then work my way along the rope stitching the netting to it. As I worked my way past the bathroom the hairs on the back of my neck stood on end! Something or someone had turned the hot water on and was running a bath. It was impossible, no-one was at home, I was alone yet it happened!

I was so spooked that I called a mate the next day. He was a heating engineer and worked for the gas board. He came around and checked the appliance to confirm that everything was in good working order.

He was not able to offer an explanation at all as to what I had witnessed.

On another occasion we actually got the police involved. The flat was in the main shopping street, Northdown Road at Cliftonville and it was above an estate agent's office. The entrance to the flat was situated at the rear of the shop and the only access to it was via an alleyway situated between two shops. One night we opened the front door and were greeted with the sound of male voices coming from the basement. There were chalky or dusty footprints leading from the cellar door to the back door of the shop. This was a locked door that separated the shop from the flat.

In all the time we were at the flat, we had never seen the cellar door open. The estate agent's was situated right next door to a Building Society and my first thoughts were that it must be some kind of a bank robbery and they were trying to gain access to next door via the cellar. We immediately left the building, made our way back to the main road and crossed it to where there was a public payphone on the corner. We telephoned the police and then waited for them before going back to the flat. At no time whatsoever did we see anyone leave the building either via the alleyway or via the estate agent's front door.

The police were very quickly on the scene and we explained to them exactly what had happened. We then took them down the alleyway and around to the front door of the flat. On entering the hallway we found that the cellar door was now closed. One of the policemen tried the handle and the door opened. He went down into the basement with his flashlight only to find there was nothing there but cobwebs. Had it not been for the chalky footprints on the hallway carpet I think the coppers would have assumed that we were either stark raving mad or wasting their time.

They followed the footprints from the cellar to the door that separated the flat from the estate agents. It was locked and the footprints did not return. The only way for the police to gain entry into the offices was to contact the owner and ask him to come down immediately. By now it was about one in the morning.

The owner arrived and unlocked the door. Much to everyone's surprise, the footprints went right through the offices and into the estate agents shop. They continued to the shop entrance and out onto the main road. To this day nobody has been able to explain how or why this had happened. The nearest I ever got to finding out about the weird goings on in the flat came from the girls who worked in the Building Society next door. I had gone in there to pay some money into my account and had happened to comment on the strange hours that their cleaner worked. I had heard bangs and crashes and furniture being dragged across the floor several times in the middle of the night.

The girls informed me that it was not the cleaner making all the noises that I had heard, it was probably the old girl that *used* to live there. She had apparently been dead for several years but some of the girls reckoned they had seen her sitting on the stairs and looking at them vacantly. I wish I could say that I had seen her, but neither myself or Teresa ever did. We never ever saw anything remotely like a ghost, a friend of mine that rented the flat when we left it was there for about five years. He never heard or experienced anything unusual at all in the time he was there.

Not the best of starts!

Fishing had been extremely poor one winter, not only had the weather been bad but the cod hadn't shown up. For some reason that I cannot explain, I ended up swapping my boat 'The Dragonfly' for a small motor yacht called 'Stella'. I had no knowledge whatsoever about sailing but thought that at some point in the future I would either teach myself how to sail or would sell it for a profit.

I kept the name that came with the boat for a couple of reasons, one being the fact that superstition around seafaring folk believe that a name change on a boat brings bad luck. The other reason was simply the fact that I liked to drink a few pints of the stuff!

She was a motor yacht of carvel construction, eighteen feet in overall length and about eight foot in the beam. She was equipped with a 7.5 hp Stuart Turner inboard engine. The main purpose for the engine would be for maneuvering around harbours and for confined spaces and mooring. Unfortunately, she was only equipped with a small foresail, for some reason the main sail was missing. She had an inbuilt compass for navigation, a hand pump for bailing out water, a couple of bunks for sleeping in and a two ring cooker with a grill.

As I said, fishing had been diabolical I worked extremely hard and worked long hours. I also worked in weather where I should have stayed ashore and all this to earn very little. Both Teresa and I were pissed off with the situation as it was and came up with a ridiculous plan to emigrate.

We would take 'Stella' and sail off into the sunset. We would navigate our way across the English Channel, once we arrived in France we would follow the coast in a south westerly direction until we reached the port of Le Havre. We would then motor up the River Seine until we reached Paris. We would motor through the French capital and onto the canal system. We would then make our way through the canals down to the Mediterranean. On arrival at the Mediterranean coast, we would soak up the sunshine and spend the summer as fruit pickers. Instead of hearing about how much greener the grass was on the other side we were actually going to go and find out for ourselves.

We spent a week or so preparing ourselves for the trip, sorting out equipment, tools and supplies etc. most importantly, we sorted out as much cash as we could and got a hold of and a top quality RAC road map of France. I can't believe I actually navigated the French coast with only this but I did.

We were ready, we were going to escape from the rut we were in, we were going to start a new life in this ill equipped 18ft motor yacht with a few of our possessions and a grand total of about four hundred quid. We couldn't see a problem with our plan but everyone else thought we were stark raving mad. They had come to the conclusion that we had lost the plot and everything was doomed to fail.

We were not going to let them put us off, we stuck to our guns and left Broadstairs harbour one morning with brilliant sunshine, a good forecast and a favourable tide. We slowly made our way along the coast to Ramsgate, past the harbour entrance and then on into Pegwell bay. We then turned to the south to head for Deal before carrying on to Dover. The plan when we got to Dover was to follow the ferries to France and tie up for the night at Calais.

Three hours into our journey, we encountered our first problem, the engine appeared to be running faster and the boat seemed to be going slower. I lifted the engine box cover off and on inspection found that the engine was running smoothly but the propeller shaft had stopped turning. I anchored up about a half mile off the coast at St Margaret's Bay to carry out an emergency repair. I drilled a small hole through the gearbox cup-link and banged a nail through it to try and link the two back together.

After doing this, I started the engine and carefully slid it into gear. Sure enough, as the cup-link rotated so did the shaft. The repair was successful, the only problem was I did not know how long it would last. We hauled the anchor and slowly made our way to Dover harbour to carry out a proper repair before continuing with our journey. We entered Dover harbour via the northern entrance and as sods law would have it, as soon as we were inside the harbour my repair gave out. Yet again we were not able to move the boat but this time we were right in the way of all the cross channel ferries.

A French ferry was blasting his horn to signal me to get out of the way, at the same time another ferry was outside the entrance waiting for Port control to let him in. A Hovercraft had to change its course to avoid a collision with the ferry on the outside and on entering the harbour had to change course again to avoid hitting us. The timetables of two ferries, somewhere between eight hundred and fifteen hundred holidaymakers and at least eighty hairy HGV drivers had been disrupted while I tried to fix the problem. Eventually, a harbour launch came over screaming abuse at me before passing us a rope to tow us out of the way and into the yacht basin.

We tied up on a pontoon and Teresa set about making something to eat. While she did this, I carried out a better repair job. I drilled a bigger hole which enabled me to put a decent size stainless nut and bolt through the cup-link and as a precaution, we bought a handful of nuts and bolts with the theory, that if it went again it would be easy to tap out the sheered bolt and replace it with a new one.

We spent the night aboard the boat at Dover, we had decided that it would be best to cross the Channel in daylight, just in case we encountered any more problems. We chatted to several other yachtsmen, they all thought we were fucking mad and the only advice they could give us was to leave Dover when the tide was running to the north and head back to Ramsgate!

From beer cans to guns

Having spent the night in the marina, we showered and had a quick breakfast before saying goodbye to some very concerned yachtsmen. I assured them that they had nothing to worry about and that we had no intention of crossing the channel. We would be taking their advice and heading straight back to Ramsgate with our tails firmly between our legs.

Upon leaving the marina, we motored towards the southern entrance of the outer harbour as we didn't want to cross the ferry berths. We then motored through the gap in the wall and out into the open sea. Once clear of the harbour I pointed the boat in an easterly direction straight for France. There was no way on earth that we were going to give up on our dream regardless of what anyone had said to us or advised us to do.

It was a beautiful day and despite making very slow progress we could see that the English coast was gradually getting smaller. We maintained an easterly course with cross channel ferries and the occasional hovercraft passing us at fairly frequent intervals. It was just as well there were plenty of ferries, I hadn't accounted for how fast they were and there was no way we could have kept up with them. After several hours we finally lost sight of the UK coastline. We continued on our course with the ferries seeming to get further and further away to the south of us. I had no way of checking the tidal flow, I didn't have a proper chart, all I had was a roadmap of France!

I started to realise what a bloody idiot I was but did not want to alarm Teresa, so I kept my thoughts to myself and just kept heading east. Logic told me that eventually I must reach the French coastline somewhere near Calais.

The sun continued to shine, the temperature got higher and higher and the sea was like a millpond. We didn't care how long it was going to take, we were on our way to start a new life. Teresa decided to take advantage of the fact that there was no one about and the sun was shining. She stripped off to just her bikini bottoms and began to sunbathe on the foredeck.

I scanned the horizon and saw that we were completely on our own and then thought to myself 'happy days, here we go'. I slowed the engine down and put the gearbox into neutral, as far as I was concerned we could just bob around for a while, I had a stirring in my groin that needed sorting out. We had a laugh and a joke around and then before long we were getting down to business.

Picture yourself in my shoes for a minute, you are in your early twenties and have left the United Kingdom in a small boat to pursue your dreams. The sun is shining, you are miles from anyone or anywhere and your girlfriend is naked. This is just the start of your dream and your whole future lay ahead of you.

Suddenly, we were interrupted by the blast of a ships horn and it frightened the shit out of me. I jumped up to see what was going on only to see the 'Sally Line' on its way from Ramsgate to Dunkirk. It passed us with about 50 yards to spare and as it went passed a load of blokes on the deck were shouting 'Give her one for us!' and throwing beer cans at us. By this time Teresa had turned crimson and crawled into the cabin to hide. I just shrugged my shoulders, waved at the blokes and gave them the thumbs up.

Apart from the embarrassing situation we found ourselves in, I was relieved to see the ferry. At least from this point I had a pretty good idea of how to get to Dunkirk. It was further to the north than we planned on being, but at least it was France. My thoughts were that the journey would be a lot easier from then on, all I had to do was follow the coast in a south-westerly direction until we reached the Seine Estuary.

The ferry quickly disappeared into the distance, so I made sure I had a decent compass bearing to follow, to ensure we got to our destination. We motored for ages and still no signs of France. Eventually we lost the daylight, what a great situation to be in, we were stuck somewhere in the English Channel with a road map and a torch to navigate with!

We maintained our course and eventually spotted a faint glow on the horizon. As we edged towards the glow it got brighter and before too long we found ourselves amongst a load of French fishing boats.

I heaved a sigh of relief when I finally found a channel marked with red and green lights showing us the way to Dunkirk Harbour. Upon entering the port we just looked for somewhere to tie up for the night. There was no point in steaming all the way to the marina as we would be off on the next leg of our journey as soon as we had had some sleep and the tide was with us. We steamed into a small creek and tied up alongside a shipwreck before getting some shut eye.

I had only been asleep for about an hour when I was woken up by the sound of dogs barking, and someone shouting things in French. I lay there for a minute trying to work out what was going on before eventually poking my head out of the cabin door. I nearly shit myself! I was greeted by a French customs officer who was glaring at me and pointing a gun straight at my head. As if that wasn't enough, he had three dogs and armed reinforcements with him.

The officer climbed aboard and took a good look around. I assumed he was looking for drugs and he quickly established that we were innocent and that he was wasting his time. He scowled, uttered something to his colleagues and then climbed off the boat. As they walked away I couldn't help thinking to myself 'is this dream of ours really such a good idea?'

Some Haircut!

Dunkirk was an absolute shit hole. It was about appealing as having a fork stuck in your eye. Apart from the incident with the customs officers there was nothing but eyesores wherever you looked. The harbour was awful, caked in thick black mud and there was rubbish everywhere from empty plastic bottles to used sanitary towels and condoms. Several rusty old ships that looked like remnants of the second world war were scattered around the outer harbour.

To top it all, there was a vile smell in the air, probably coming from huge industrial units that had been constructed in the area. These buildings had like a pipe rising from them and flames were burning on the top of them. Dense pungent smoke was drifting across the skyline, making it very hazy and giving the atmosphere a kind of green poisonous tinge to it. It was very depressing and to this day I cannot understand why someone would want to live there.

Fortunately, it was not long before the tide started ebbing and we were able to leave and continue with our journey. I started up, untied our ropes and then headed out of the harbour and out into the open sea again. As we edged along the land the scenery became much more pleasant and we left the industrial eyesore behind.

We saw some beautiful beaches with grass patches and big sand dunes. Before long, Calais loomed into view which gave me confirmation that we had plenty of tide with us. Bearing this in mind and knowing that we were behind schedule I steamed straight past the harbour and headed on towards Bologne. This was always going to be a port of call, I had been there several times and knew that we could moor up right next to the shops and bars.

We arrived at Bologne, entered the harbour and then motored up to where the fishing boats tied up. The plan was to tie up with them and avoid the marina and the harbour fees! From where the fishing boats moored it was only a few hundred metres to the supermarket. We bought a few basics such as bread and eggs and I took the opportunity to fill up our jerry can. We had used a lot more fuel than expected on our longer than expected crossing the previous day.

Once the shopping was done and we re-fuelled, we took to the streets to find a phone box and call home to let everyone know we were OK. We then grabbed a change of clothes and our wash bags and sneaked into the Marina shower block to get cleaned up. We spent a very relaxing evening in Bologne and even managed to get ten hours sleep. We woke yet again to brilliant sunshine and as we did the previous day, and we left with the tide ebbing to the south west. We were going to make a short trip along the coast and according to my roadmap Valery-Sur-Somme was to be our next port of call. We arrived safely and after travelling a couple of miles inland on the river found some moorings for the afternoon and evening.

We left this lovely place the next morning and did the same as the previous day the only difference being Treport was our next stopping point. After sleeping at Treport we made our way to Dieppe. The Harbour at Dieppe was quite commercial, it had a lot of larger fishing vessels and there was also a ferry that crossed the channel to Newhaven. Unfortunately, we were unable to tie up with the fishing boats and had no choice other than to tie up with the other yachts in the marina. The marina was rammed with boats, the only space I could find was next to a gleaming motor yacht. It was about 45 to 50 feet in length and could only be described as a rich man's toy. The wheelhouse had all sorts of fancy gadgets in it and on the stern there was a small boat complete with outboard hung gracefully from a stainless steel pivot.

I hung several old tyres over the side of our boat so as to not scratch the side of the yacht. We were ushered away by the bloke on board who ran inside his cabin to go and get some white fenders for us to lie alongside. He obviously did not want any dirty tyre marks along the side of his gleaming gin palace! Once I secured the boat, we were invited aboard for drinks. This was the life, a vintage malt whiskey out of a crystal de-canter.

Several whiskeys later, he had a horrified look on his face when I jumped back on board our boat and returned with the roadmap to show him our plans. he was speechless for a while before uttering to us that we could not continue our journey without a proper sea chart. He then rummaged through one of the drawers in the wheelhouse and dug out a chart. It had just gone out of date and he had himself a replacement. He insisted we took it and was absolutely gobsmacked that we had got as far as we had on a roadmap.

That evening we ate dinner with him and during our conversation Teresa told him she was a hairdresser. To this day I have no idea whether he was being serious or just polite, but it turned out he wanted a haircut and asked Teresa if she would cut it. She agreed, and she suggested doing it on the pontoon rather than getting loose hair all over his lovely cabin. She grabbed her comb and scissors and they both climbed over the rail and onto the pontoon. Whilst she was getting ready, I poured myself another large whiskey and filled it with ice. I could not in a million years have imagined what happened next, in fact it was unbelievable. I was looking on, scotch in hand on this lovely boat, and Teresa walked along the pontoon a few metres and picked up a hosepipe that was attached to a tap. The hosepipe had some sort of fitting on the end and it looked like some sort of high pressure attachment.

Before I could warn her, she turned the tap on with the hose aimed at the back of his head. The water came out with so much force it hit him on the back of his head and sent him flying off the pontoon and into the marina! He shrieked as he realised what had happened, he was spluttering and spitting out this horrible salty water he had swallowed whilst trying to climb back onto the pontoon. Meanwhile, I was aboard his luxury yacht with a finest malt whiskey in hand thinking to myself 'Jesus Christ Teresa you fucked up there!'

A good job we were not Muslim!

On the whole life was getting better, we were constantly meeting new people and everyone wanted to help us. The weather remained good and we were quickly forgetting about how hard it had been at home, struggling to make a living and paying the bills. We had no urgency to get anywhere and didn't pay any attention to our rapidly dwindling funds. The next harbour we stopped at was in a place called St Valery-en-Caux before moving on to a place called Fecamp.

The harbours and the scenery seemed to be getting prettier as we edged our way to the west. Fecamp was definitely our favourite to date and we stayed there for a couple of nights before making our way to Le Havre. The plan was to stock up there before making our way across the estuary and then head inland up the river Seine towards Paris. We were in for a big shock when we arrived at Le Havre, it was huge, it stretched for miles. There were massive cranes and sets of heavy lifting gear on huge concrete quays for as far as the eye could see. Huge ships were being unloaded and other Trans-Atlantic container ships were moored in the estuary waiting to be unloaded. They were like huge blocks of flats as we passed them by it even seemed to get darker as the sun disappeared behind them.

We had no idea of where to go, but fortunately there was a constant stream of yachts making their way up a green and red buoyed channel towards the town. We did the obvious thing and followed them and eventually ended up in a yacht basin. There were plenty of facilities there, from shower blocks to duty free shops to clubs and restaurants. Despite the facilities that were there, we had already made our mind up that we would only be there for the one night. It was a horribly overcrowded place, there was a horrible stench of diesel and to make matters worse everything was bloody expensive. We did our shopping, fuelled up, got a reasonable night's sleep and left on the morning tide.

I worked out that the tide would push us upstream as I motored south towards the other side of the estuary. Le Havre was so big it seemed to take forever to get out of the harbour. We eventually did and made our way to a place called Honfleur which was our next planned stop. On arrival there we found the lock gates open wide so we motored straight into the marina which turned out to be right in the middle of the town. We were surrounded by cafes and restaurants, all with outside seating and this was the case wherever you chose to tie up.

We moored up and eagerly went ashore to have a look around. The place was stunning, it was one of them places where you couldn't walk past an estate agents window without having a nose. The houses were mega bucks, and to top it all the beer prices were nearly double the price we had been paying elsewhere. Despite the prices we stayed there for four nights. I had figured out that now we were heading inland our money would go a lot further. Not only would I be using the tide to push us towards Paris, we would not be paying anymore mooring fees as I would just tie the boat up on the riverbank.

On the day of our departure we took the boat out of the marina before they closed the lock gates and then we moored up outside to wait for the tide to drop to its lowest point. We watched lumps of weed flow past us towards the sea and eventually they slowed down and stopped. This was our time to make a move. We untied and headed inland with our speed seeming to increase all the time. I have no idea how much tide there was but in a very short space of time there was plenty of it!

Things were going great, we were making a lot of headway when all of a sudden there was a blast from a ships horn. I looked behind me and couldn't believe the size of the ship that was steaming up on us, it was huge, in fact it was hard to believe that a ship this size could even get up a river. I managed to get out of his way, and from then on made a decision to hog the riverbank and keep out of the way of any other ships that we might encounter. Loads of ships passed us at regular intervals and they were all heading in the same direction as us.

The tide quickly slowed down eventually coming to a halt and we found somewhere safe to moor up for the rest of the day. By the time we had cooked some grub the tide was screaming the other way. There was now a constant stream of ships running in the opposite direction. We had clearly made the right decision to stop when we did.

The next day we caught the early tide and continued with our journey. After a while we motored into the port of Rouen. It was an awful place, very industrialized with a smell that was worse than Le Havre. The river was full of oil and chemicals and there were dead and rotten fish floating everywhere for as far as the eye could see. It was that bad that 'Greenpeace' were there with their flagship the Rainbow Warrior carrying out an international protest.

Our plan had been to stay there for the night but we quickly abandoned that idea and continued with our journey. We used the last of the tide and then dropped anchor to await the next tide. We made do with what food we had and drank gallons of tea. Eventually, some six hours later we found ourselves underway again. It was quite late in the day and my main concern was the darkness that lay ahead and finding somewhere to stop for the night. The daylight soon disappeared and a full moon came out. It was easy to follow the river by the moonlight so despite not having any navigation lights I decided to keep going. We motored until about eleven and then came across a pontoon. We tied up for the night. It had been an extremely long day and we had run out of food hours ago.

Not far from where we had moored there was a building with some lights on so we decided to go over there and investigate. What a result!! It was a bar and there were still a couple of people in it. Communicating with them was our next problem, they couldn't understand a word of English and they didn't seem to understand my very amateurish French either.

With a bit of makeshift sign language we soon got them to understand that we wanted to eat and drink. They beckoned us to sit at a table and they brought us fresh coffee and beer. They followed that by serving us up some lovely thick French bread and a plate of meat stuff. We had no idea what it was, we were hungry and we didn't care and in any case it tasted good.

The couple that owned the bar came and joined us and despite the language barrier we laughed and joked until about four in the morning. During the time we were there I was desperate to find out what we had eaten. Finally, with the aid of a dictionary I got them a pencil and paper and asked them to draw it for me.

 I don't know what Teresa was expecting, but I was pretty convinced it was going to be a rabbit or possibly a horse. After all we were in France and I had heard that they ate that sort of stuff all the time. He finished his drawing and past it to me. I looked at it with amazement, he had drawn a picture of a pig's head and it turned out that that was exactly what we had eaten. Just imagine if we had been Muslim!

Decision time

The following day we woke up to find that the weather had turned for the worse. The sky was no longer a bright blue, it had become very overcast and there was that horrible fine drizzle in the air. Fortunately, neither of us suffered any after effects of any description that could have been caused by the consumption of the pigs head the night before or for that matter the amount of French lager we had consumed so the decision was made to get underway early.

Teresa counted up our finances including all the loose change and it became very apparent that they had shrunk at an alarming rate. We had been reasonably careful with our spending but were down to about a hundred and thirty quid. We originally thought when we first set sail from Broadstairs that we would have made it to the south of France by now and would be getting paid for picking some sort of exotic fruit in the Mediterranean sunshine.

How wrong we were, we had not even made it to Paris and that was only about a third of the inland journey. We had clearly not allowed anywhere near enough to cover our fuel costs. The problem with the cup-link that we had been plagued with on the early part of our journey recurred and forced us to make an unwanted stop. I carried out a repair as best as I could, but unfortunately the time taken to do this meant I had missed the bloody tide. We spent the next six hours pacing up and down the riverbank pulling our hair out. The tide finally turned in our favour and we got underway again with the intention of at least getting to Paris before we made another stop.

We motored along the river and into the midnight hours. It was quite difficult to navigate in the dark but we were at the point of no return. We made slow but steady progress, winding our way along the river for as long as we could. A combination of poor visibility and a turn of the tide yet again forced us to make another unwanted stop. By the time we found somewhere to tie up it was about three in the morning. I climbed into the bunk absolutely shattered and very frustrated as well. It had been an extremely long day, we used a load of fuel, our gas bottle had run out and there was still no sign whatsoever of Paris getting any closer.

Just about everything had gone pear shaped and after discussing everything over a makeshift breakfast we agreed that the party was over. We had no choice other than to make a u turn and head for home. The only thing we could do was to make a stop at the nearest place we could, have a proper meal, buy gas and fuel, and stock up on provisions. We set off, this time downstream and a couple of hours later pulled in at a small village and did what had to be done.

Finally, with hot food inside us, fuel, gas and basic shopping we set off. We were travelling in silence, neither of us wanting to make conversation, basically, we were both pissed off. It had been good fun whilst it lasted, but suddenly we had been brought back to earth with a bang and were on our way home.

I did exactly the same as on the inland leg of our journey and used the tide to help us on our way only this time we were travelling towards the sea. There was something that kept niggling me, and it didn't matter what I tried to think about it wouldn't go away. It was the fact that everyone back home had told us we were mad in the first place to attempt the journey and they would be queuing up to remind us of that fact on our return.

We made a few stops back to the coast, one of them being the place where we ate the pigs head. We explained as best we could our predicament to them and were quick to get underway again as time and money were not on our side. We motored into the darkness yet again and finally reached the Port of Rouen. The lights from the town and the harbour coupled up with the lights from the ships moored up were ample for me to see where we were going so we just kept on motoring. A day or so later we found ourselves back at Honfleur. We had to tie up outside the marina as the tide was low and the lock gates were closed. When the tide had risen enough the gates opened and we entered the marina. We planned to spend the night here before motoring across the estuary and back up the coast to Calais.

We had a good night out, trying to make the most of the holiday atmosphere for the last time. We ate well, drank loads of beer and wine and finished off with a good night's sleep. When we woke up, we had breakfast cast our ropes off and headed out into the open sea. Fortunately, the weather was good with hardly any breeze and plenty of sunshine. Across the estuary we could clearly make out Le Havre and the journey looked pretty straight forward as there were plenty of container ships both arriving and departing from the harbour to point out the way to us.

I felt like I had failed and was really reluctant to head north. I finally turned to Teresa who had hardly said a word and said something like 'Bollocks to this, I am not ready to go home yet. I reckon we can head the other way and make it to Jersey before the fuel and money runs out. I think they speak English there so it should be easy to find a job. Make a decision in the next five minutes and tell me which way you want me to go.' She looked at me and smiled and then as I expected said 'If you think we can make it to Jersey crack on because I am not ready to go home yet either'

Mussels, mussels and more mussels

We motored west for a while before the coastline turned towards the south west. We altered course and followed the coastline staying about a mile offshore. Later that day we pulled into a small river like estuary with a town on each side. One side was Deauville and the other was Trouville. We moored up and stayed the night and it was here that I had a brainwave. I had thought of a great way to cut down on our food expenses. Teresa could go to the shops and buy some French bread an onion and a cheap bottle of wine, and whilst she was out shopping I would go down the beach and collect some fresh mussels off the rocks that we had passed on our way into the harbour. All we had to do then was slice the onion, put it in a saucepan of wine, bring it to the boil and cook the mussels in it. This we did, and hey Presto we had moules mariniere at virtually no cost whatsoever.

We ate the mussels, mopped our plates clean with the bread and then opted to stay on board so that we could not be tempted to buy anything. We played cards for a few hours and then turned in so that we could get an early start in the morning.

The following day we had really good weather again so by seven o clock we had left the harbour and were underway again. We kept heading west with a few uneventful days, stopping at Ouisterham and Grandcamp on the way. Moules mariniere became the order of the day whenever and wherever it was possible to pick a bucket of them. This was saving us loads of money which we knew we needed for fuel. Whilst we were moored at Grandcamp the weather took a turn for the worse with the wind picking up to a good force six from the west. Fortunately for us we were at the south eastern corner of the Cherbourg peninsula and by keeping tight into the land were able to make our way north despite the bad weather to the port of Barfleur.

On arrival there we had to make a stop for several reasons. One was to get more fuel, but the other reason was far more concerning, the poor weather was stopping us from proceeding any further. There was no way we would be able to continue across the top of the peninsular until either the wind had eased back or it swung around to the south. We were stuck there for three days before I decided to make a move.

Against advice from several locals (including the harbour master) we left the harbour on an ebbing tide in a bid to motor around the coast to Cherbourg and at least be one step closer to Jersey. It wasn't long before we were in real trouble and we found ourselves surrounded by raging white water that was breaking all over the place. I had deliberately left with the tide in our favour to help us on our way, which was great apart from the fact that the wind which was still strong was in the opposite direction.

I got to the stage where I couldn't continue any further, the waves were far too big, and the boat was struggling to cope with them. I managed to safely turn the boat around only to find that the current was far too strong to be able to get back to Barfleur. We were in shit street, it was a scary and dangerous situation we were in. I attempted to make headway in both directions several times but every time it was to no avail.

Finally, I insisted that Teresa put a life jacket on and then desperately tried to get the attention of a French fishing boat that was working nearby. I waved frantically at them and then to my horror they waved back at me! I tried shouting to them, they couldn't hear me because the wind was carrying my voice off in the wrong direction. I then started thinking that they were also in difficulties, they had been doing the same as I had, first going in one direction and then turning and then repeating their movements over and over again.

We were like two boats copying each other and doing the same thing about a third of a mile apart. Our bilge pump was doing overtime, there was a lot more water coming on board than we could clear. Eventually, after about an hour I saw the French boat turn and head over towards us. They threw us a rope which we gratefully accepted and then they slowly towed us out of the white water and safely back into Barfleur. It is difficult to explain how I felt at the time, but to say I was relieved would be a gross understatement. Truth be known, I am surprised I didn't shit myself.

Back on dry land I thanked the people who had rescued us and asked them as best I could why they had not come straight over to us when I waved at them. It turned out that they thought I was drifting through the rapids fishing for bass and had no idea at first that we were in trouble!

This latest episode had just about finished Teresa off and she packed her holdall. I asked her what she was doing to which she replied 'I have had fuck all to eat apart from Mussels for the last four days, I feel like I am lucky to be alive after today and I have had enough. I am going to find the train station and I am going home'. With her outburst over, she climbed off the boat taking her holdall with her and headed off towards the town. There wasn't much I could do about it so let her go and made myself some hot tea. I then went off to collect some mussels for my dinner. On my return to the boat she was on board, she hadn't changed her mind but had found out that the next train going in the direction of home was not for another three days! She had calmed down by now and set about cooking yet more moules mariniere. Nice as they were, we were sick of them, there are limits to how long you can eat them. Fortunately, we had both escaped any problems with food poisoning or the runs, you would have thought with the amount we had eaten that we would have been shitting through the eye of a needle by now.

 A few days later the weather changed for the better and we set sail and arrived safely at Cherbourg where we pulled in to wait for the tide to turn in our favour. The last leg of the French coast was to be the 'Alderney Race' where the current can run at up to eight knots and there is a 40ft rise and fall in the tide. Several boats left Cherbourg at the same time and once outside the harbour headed west. We followed them and when we reached the north west tip of the peninsular I altered course to the south and headed towards

Carterat which was to be our last stop before the short crossing to Jersey.

We were the only boat following the coast, the other boats had headed much further west before swinging to the south as it was the safest route to take. We hadn't been able to do this as we had not got enough fuel. All I could do was to try and avoid any white water as this would be where the rocks were. We safely navigated the 'Race' and successfully made it to Carterat. Unfortunately, we ran aground on the way into the harbour as the tide was out, but as soon as the tide started rising again we headed into the harbour and moored up alongside a visitor's pontoon.

A local fishing boat returned to port and the crew started unloading their catch. I went over to them and helped them unload and they rewarded me with a decent spider crab. I took it back to the boat and we joked about it being shellfish but not mussels before cooking it and tucking in.

There's no work here, mate

The next morning Teresa threw off the ropes, I pushed the boat away from the harbour wall and we slowly headed out of Carterat with Jersey in full view to the west of us. I had calculated that it would take us about three hours to get there. We had run out of money completely and were down to less than a third of a tank of fuel. Things were tight but with good weather and a slack tide I was pretty sure we could make it.

We motored for about an hour and the sea started to change colour indicating to me that it was getting a lot shallower. I turned to the south and followed a rocky reef until it appeared to stop and then I swung back around to the west. A short time later I could make out a castle on a hill and it appeared to have harbour lights below it. I didn't know at the time where we were heading for, but it turned out to be the port of Gorey. It seemed to take us forever, I dipped the tank a few times to see how much fuel we had left and it got to the stage where it was not even registering on the piece of wood I was using.

We entered the harbour, I took a quick look around and spotted a couple of registered fishing boats which would be ideal to tie alongside and as I headed towards them the engine coughed and spluttered and died. The boat glided slowly over to them and I managed to secure a rope before saying to Teresa 'How fucking close was that!'

We made our way ashore, we were absolutely penniless but relieved, at least we were safely on dry land and in a place where they spoke English. I walked over to a couple of guys that were repairing a trawl on the quay and asked them if there were any boats looking for a crew. To my dismay they laughed and told me there was no chance of finding work anywhere in Jersey. We chatted for a while, checked with them that it would be OK to leave our boat where it was for a couple of hours, and headed off towards a row of buildings. It was quite busy, with pubs, shops, restaurants and crowds of people. There is nothing worse than seeing people drinking beer and eating fine food and knowing that your pockets are empty. As we approached the end of the buildings a familiar sight appeared. We both spotted it at the same time and we almost broke out into a run. Sure enough, it was a Barclays Bank and it was open. Teresa had an account with Barclays in Margate and she was pretty sure there was still about twenty quid in it.

We went to the counter and they confirmed that we could cash a cheque there. In no time at all we had changed from being destitute to what felt like Christmas day. We left the bank and rushed back to the boat to get the cheque book. We returned to the bank, checked the balance which turned out to be just over eighteen quid and drew out fifteen of it. We treated ourselves to sausage and chips and a beer, and then caught a bus to St Helier where we hoped the work prospects would be better. On arrival at St Helier harbour I asked around to find out where the local fishermen drank. We were given directions to a pub called 'La Folie'

We found it and went in. It was packed solid, we went to the bar and ordered a couple of drinks and then started to eavesdrop on people's conversations. It soon became clear that there was a big fishing community here. I was feeling a bit uncomfortable, I was wearing a pair of silky shorts, a tee shirt, a pair of flip flops and was about to ask for a job on a Jersey crabber. I managed to pluck up the courage and ask if anyone knew of anybody that needed a crew but got a negative response. They seemed to find my request quite amusing, and one guy in particular took the piss out of me. We kept ourselves to ourselves and put up with the situation for about ten to fifteen minutes. In the end I went up to the guy that was coming out with all the sarcastic comments and asked him if I could have a word with him outside. The pub fell silent and I could feel the eyes in the back of my head as I walked outside with this bloke following me.

Once we were outside it was easy to take control of the situation, I made it perfectly clear that I was not looking for any trouble and then went on to tell him the predicament we were in. I then explained to him that I was in fact a fisherman from Kent in South

East England. We chatted for a while and then he ushered me over to the quayside. He pointed to a boat on the opposite quay and told me that the bloke was sailing at six in the morning and was short of a second crew member. The two of us then made our way back to the bar, I shook his hand and he confirmed that he would telephone the bloke and let him know I would be there. We then left to catch the bus back to Gorey.

I spoke with the bus driver and asked him what time the first bus was in the morning only to find out it was not until seven o clock! I was stuffed, no bus, no money for a taxi and a job to start at six in the morning that was about six miles away. Back at Gorey I spotted a cycle hire place. I went over and found the guy in charge and told him about the situation I was in. I pointed out where we were moored up and literally begged him to loan me a bike until I got paid. He reluctantly agreed to my request and we left with a bike to sort out some work clothes and knock up a packed lunch. I went to bed early so as that I would be fresh the next day to start work.

Working in Jersey

I woke up at 04.50 wondering just what I had let myself in for, I had a quick cup of tea and then cycled to St Helier to attempt to impress this bloke and get myself a permanent job. I arrived early, the skipper and another guy called Louis turned up at about a quarter to six and they seemed surprised that I had actually made it. I introduced myself and we climbed aboard to go fishing for the day. I had been a commercial fishing off the Kent coast for several years but had not done much in the way of lobster potting. Most of my fishing had been done with static nets for cod and skate. Fortunately, I had forty pots which I used to use along the coastline close to home. I had made them up into four strings of ten and I used to haul them every other day. This had made me feel confident that I would be able to do the job. The skipper, a guy called Willy Marsh asked me what experience I had, and to impress him I told him I worked 80 pots split down into eight strings of ten.

He gave me a strange look and said 'We have got eighty pots on a string and we have eight strings of them to do!' I shrugged my shoulders and didn't say anything, I assumed he was on a wind up, after all it would not be possible to do 640 pots in a day. After about an hour and a half of steaming south we arrived at the fishing grounds and proceeded to haul the first string. I was on the gunnel, otherwise known as the rail, lifting the pots aboard and emptying the crab and lobster before passing them to Louis who baited them and then stacked them three high along the length of the boat. He then started a second row, I couldn't believe it, we went past thirty and then passed forty and then fifty. Sixty came aboard and still I couldn't see the other end. I thought 'Fuck me this bloke isn't joking' After seventy I spotted the end and sure enough, by the time we got there we had eighty pots on board.

I was just about to light a fag when I heard the skipper shout 'Go'. Louis carefully rolled the pots back to me in the correct order, with my job being to pick them up and throw them over the side. The pots were flying at me, we were shooting them at about seven knots! I had never seen anything like it, I was sweating buckets and in less than forty minutes we had hauled, baited, stacked and shot eighty lobster pots. The day progressed and it was getting harder and harder, I could feel myself really starting to struggle. After five strings they asked me if I was ready to go home. Being in the situation that I was in and desperately needing this job I replied 'I thought we had eight strings to do, lets crack on and do the lot'

We went on to complete the day and then headed back to port. I felt like I was dying, I was absolutely fucked, I had back ache like I had never experienced before and if it hadn't been for my pride I would have literally crawled off the boat on my hands and knees. Once ashore, the boss stuck his hand in his pocket pulled out some cash and handed me thirty quid. (That is a lot of money when you are broke) He then went on to say 'If you are here at six in the morning the job is yours' to which I confirmed that I would be and thanked him for my wages. They said goodbye and left me sat on the harbour wall. I was there for a good half hour trying to muster up the energy to cycle back to Gorey.

I peddled back to the boat, very pleased with myself and eager to tell Teresa the good news. Once back at the boat I was surprised to find that she wasn't there. I looked around but there was no sign of her. Off came my boots and on went the kettle and I made myself a sandwich. About half an hour passed and Teresa returned with a big grin on her face. Whilst I had been fishing, she had been off for a wander and managed to get a job selling ice-cream in a kiosk for £15 a session. Even better was the fact that it was only about 200 yards from where the boat was moored.

 The thought that was going around in both of our heads was the conversation that we had had with the fisherman the day before on the quayside when we had been told quite clearly that there was no work in Jersey! There is always work if you want it bad enough.

Ice-cream or steak

Every morning I got up at five, had cereal and tea and then cycled into St Helier to go out on the boat. Teresa would get up later, tidy the boat up and do any odd jobs or shopping that was needed. In the afternoon she would make her way to the ice-cream kiosk at the 'Drive-In BBQ'

I came home on the Friday evening to find Teresa on the boat and not at the kiosk. She was clearly upset about something and it was obvious from her eyes that she had been crying. I asked her what was wrong, and she told me that everything had gone pear shaped at work. The owner had been in a foul mood because the weather had been poor with a load of rain and this had kept the customers away. To top it all, the ice-cream machine had grunted and groaned before exploding and packing up. This had resulted in Teresa getting smothered in ice-cream (If I had been there when it had happened I would have been dying of laughter) and the owner refusing to pay her. He had grinned at her and smugly said that there was nothing she could do about it as she didn't have a work permit and shouldn't have been there in the first place.

Before I continue, it is necessary for me to explain what this bloke was like. He was originally from London and had decided to set up home and business in Jersey. It was clear from his business venture and his home that he was worth a few quid. It was just as well, because he had nothing else going for him. My thoughts regarding his personality were later proven by some local people who informed me that a few years earlier he had gone to Asia to buy himself a wife as it was the only way he could get one! He was big headed and arrogant, and to top it all, he was built like a brick shit house. He must have stood six feet four and he was very broad across the shoulders. He had piercing blue eyes, blond hair and a double chin, someone that would have made Adolph proud.

Anyway, getting back to where I was, I had been paid for the week and I told her not to worry about it. I suggested that we could go there later that evening, chill out, have something to eat and then have a chat to him about her wages. She agreed, so we showered and sorted out clean clothes and then headed over to the 'Drive-In BBQ' at about eight o clock. We found a nice secluded table for two and sat down to eat. I can't remember what Teresa had, but I distinctly remember having a prawn cocktail for my starter. I then ordered sirloin steak with mushrooms and all the trimmings for my main course.

We both had a fantastic meal with the steak cooked to perfection and this was coupled with a few beers. It must have been about ten thirty by the time we had finished our dessert and the place was really buzzing with people out for the night. The waiter came over and handed me the bill and then to Teresa's astonishment I put my plan into action. I pointed to the boss and said 'tell him to take it out of her wages'. The waiter was confused and asked me to repeat myself which I did. Teresa was staring at me and I could tell by her expression that she was not amused at what I was doing.

The waiter walked over to his boss, said something to him and that is when the shit hit the fan and I mean hit the fan. He stormed over to me looking like a fucking psychopath. He was sending chairs flying and knocking peoples drinks over he was in such a rage. I had no chance, he was twice my size and ready to explode. God knows how high his blood pressure was, but he had so many veins sticking out of his neck and forehead it made him look like he was made of spaghetti.

He was the typical bully type of person, but due to his size I don't think he had found himself in this kind of situation before. He literally picked me up and threw me across the yard like a rag doll. I landed and staggered backwards about six paces before falling into a table of four people enjoying an evening of lobsters and wine. Their food and drink went everywhere, with much of it, noticeably a carafe of red wine spilling onto a well to do lady's lap. She was clearly very upset, it looked like her lovely white outfit was ruined and this Neanderthal type bloke was doing nothing to impress her. I remember thinking to myself 'this is going to hurt you, right in the pocket.' I also remember thinking 'I don't care what you say or do, I am not going to pay my bill'

Not only was he screaming and shouting at me, he was using foul language and he was upsetting his customers. I just taunted him, it was easy because he had lost control. It was like taking candy from a baby, I egged him on and said something like 'Well done, I bet you don't see them again' His blood was boiling, never mind the ice-cream machine exploding, I thought he was going to.

His drive-in BBQ was in an absolute mess, there were chairs everywhere, a barbeque had been knocked over and people were walking out without paying. Just think, he had ended up with all this grief because he thought he was big enough to take advantage of people. I remember him shouting for someone to call the police and agreeing with him.' Yes,' I shouted, 'call the police because I have just been assaulted'

Obviously, he did not want the police involved as he had physically attacked me so they were never called. I apologised to the people that were still there, and we left. A regular customer came after us, he caught us up and explained that anyone who committed or was seen to commit an offence on the island was immediately deported. He then offered to give me the money to be able to settle the bill. I declined his offer, showed him that I had the money and explained to him why I hadn't paid it in the first place.

Back at the boat I remember thinking to myself 'We have only been in Jersey a week and already someone has had to explain to me how easy it is to get deported!' What an eventful evening we had, and all because Teresa had not been paid and some ice-cream and a steak.

The Refund

Shortly after the incident at the Drive-in Teresa started work at a hairdresser's and she also got a couple of shifts behind the bar in the Folie. She made several friends outside of the fishing circle and introduced me to a couple she had met whilst working at the hairdresser's. Ricky was a printer with the Jersey Evening Post and his wife Caroline was a hairdresser at the same salon. Ricky found us a place to rent at Havre-des-Pas and they helped us to move in. It was like luxury to be able to sleep in a proper bed rather than being cramped up on the boat. It was also a lot closer to St Helier which made it so much easier for both of us to get to work. I continued to fish with Willy and Caroline helped Teresa turn her job from being part time to a full time post.

The hairdressers was situated in a shopping precinct in a small village called Redhouses and Teresa had to catch the bus to get there. It wasn't long before we had £200 put by to invest in a car. We bought an old Austin 1100 with an automatic gearbox. It was an awful car, but it didn't matter, it didn't go very fast and the speed limit on the island was only 30 mph anyway. On a plus side it started every time you put the key in the ignition and it got us from A to B.

 I woke up one morning after a heavy night and made myself a mug of tea before waking Teresa and leaving for work. I walked to the harbour nursing a hangover to find the boats covered in a blanket of fog. We decided to go for breakfast and wait for it to clear. We strolled to the café on the quay and ate some grub and drank gallons of tea. We waited for at least an hour and a half before deciding that the fog was set in for the day. One of the other fishermen, a guy named Phil suggested that we caught a plane and went on the piss in Guernsey. I had not been there before so I was well up for it. It certainly sounded like a much better idea than fishing in the fog with a hangover. I was unable to contact Teresa to let her know what we were up to so decided a souvenir from Guernsey would keep her sweet. Three of us agreed to go and we jumped in a cab for the airport.

At the terminal we entered the building and made our way to the 'Aurigny' desk. We purchased day return tickets which were about seventeen quid each and then headed for the bar to grab a quick beer before we departed. A couple of pints and twenty minutes later our flight number was called. We downed our drinks and made our way to the departure gate. Our tickets were checked and stamped and then a stewardess escorted us to a strange looking yellow aircraft. Once on board I was surprised at how small it was, it only had seating for about fifteen people and there was only a thin curtain separating us from the pilot. The stewardess, an extremely attractive woman did a little dance and the usual safety procedures and then requested that we all buckled up. The pilot poked his head out from behind the curtain, welcomed us aboard and then fired up the engines. Two were on the wings and a third was built into the tail section. I watched him check his instruments, radio the control tower and then slowly taxi to the runway. He accelerated down the runway and took off with what seemed like a very steep climb. He then turned sharply to the north and in a matter of minutes we were flying over the island of Sark.

Shortly after that we were over Guernsey and the stewardess advised us that the pilot was unable to land due to dense fog. The island hoppers as they were known were not equipped with radar and therefore could not guarantee a safe landing. The pilot circled the island for about forty minutes before apologising to the passengers and then headed back to Jersey. Once back on the ground we were given tickets for complimentary drinks at the bar and told to listen out for further announcements.

 What a result, a day off work and free drinks thrown in! We drank as much as we could get away with until our flight was called again. After about an hour our flight was called and fifteen minutes later we resumed our journey to Guernsey. Everything was exactly the same as the first flight, the stewardess did her little dance, the pilot took off and then veered to the north and on arrival at Guernsey the fog shut in again preventing us from landing. We got the same apology and returned to Jersey again. Once back on the ground we entered the terminal building to be given drink and food vouchers and sent to the bar again.

We had really got the taste by now, my hangover had gone and we were taking advantage of the situation. We had made friends with all the other passengers and a drinking competition evolved with chasers and just about anything else you could think of. A couple of hours later we finally got the announcement to board the plane again. We staggered on to the plane and for the third time we witnessed the stewardess do her little dance and the pilot take off.

We reached our destination only to find that the fog had returned yet again preventing us from landing. We headed back to Jersey and we head the pilot mutter something about the fucking fog doing his head in. Once back on the ground and back in the terminal an announcement was made that all flights for the remainder of the day were going to be cancelled. We were sent back to the 'Aurigny' desk where we were given an apology and offered alternative dates or a full refund of our fare. We opted for the refund as we had no idea when we would be able to go again.

To sum everything up, we had spent the whole day enjoying the views of Jersey and Corbiere lighthouse from the air, we had made some new friends, we had been treated to lunch and we had drunk a huge quantity of alcohol at no expense whatsoever. We had had a free day out!

Life Saving Equipment

I worked for a couple of years with a guy called Dougie Ward and Louis on the 'Venus II'. We all pitched in and made the job as easy as we could with me and Louis alternating the deck work from the rail to the stacking.

I am not sure what the scheme was called in Jersey, but in England it was called the 'Youth Opportunity Program' and to cut a long story short, Dougie agreed to take along a sixteen year old lad for a week so that he could gain some knowledge and experience of the fishing industry. I can't remember the lads name, but he turned up on time complete with a pack lunch and a change of clothes with him. I had been the victim of so many practical jokes on the Jersey boats and so had plenty of others and decided on this occasion that it was my turn to instigate one. Unfortunately for our newcomer he was going to be the victim of my prank.

We cast the ropes off and headed out towards the fishing grounds. Dougie was steering us out of the harbour and Louis was busy making the tea. I was getting organised at the stern of the boat cutting up the bait for the day. I beckoned the lad over to me and explained to him that we were in for a very dangerous day's work. I advised him that in the interests of safety he would have to have a large fender strapped to his back. I then went on to explain that if he fell over the side or got his foot caught in the gear he would float on the surface and we would be able to retrieve him from the sea. The poor bastard hadn't been to sea before and seemed very appreciative that I was concerned for his welfare.

With tears in my eyes I strapped a big sausage fender to his back. It was hilarious, all he needed was a pair of flippers and a mask and you would have thought he was a scuba diver. Thank god he never went over the side, he would have ended up in the water face down and would probably have drowned. Louis came out with the teas and had to turn away. I thought for a minute that he was going to wet himself. The only thing left to do now was to get Dougie's attention so that he could get on the VHF radio and share the prank with all the other day boats.

The 'Venus II' had an aft wheelhouse so I decided to send this lad up to the bow of the boat to get me a length of rope. By doing this he would be in full view of Dougie in the wheelhouse. He spotted him and then disappeared from view, he was doubled up with stomach pains he was laughing so much. The boat ended up going around in circles. One minute we had Sark on our port side, and the next minute it was on the starboard side. We seemed to be going around in circles for ages and ages until Dougie finally got his act back together and got behind the wheel to get us back on the right course.

We finally got to where the gear was and got straight to work. It was hard going, we were racing through the pots as fast as possible and we were weak with laughter. I don't know how we did it, but we managed to do the lot, even with this lad strutting about with a fender on his back. We made the poor sod wear it all day, even when we arrived back at our mooring in St Helier.

We were greeted with howls of laughter from the other fishermen. Everyone thought it was hilarious apart from a chap on the quay that I had not seen before. It turned out to be our new recruits dad, and he had come down the harbour to see how his sons first day had gone. He collected his son, accused us all of being a bunch of wankers and then stormed off down the quay. As was expected, the lad never showed up for work the next day, in fact we never saw or heard from him again.

Headcase

We had certainly settled well in Jersey and we had made loads of friends. Teresa continued with her bar work in the Folie along with her hairdressing job and I drank in the place every day after we had finished work. The number of people in there varied considerably and depended on the tides. The day boats were in there all the time and the channel boats which had four or five crew on them were in there over the big tides and away for about nine days at a time over the slacker tides.

The channel boats used to fish somewhere north of Alderney in the English Channel. The crews on these boats were re-known for working their bollocks off whilst at sea and equally re-known for their antics when ashore over the spring tides. It seemed like they had to try and spend their wages (which were very good) during their four or five days off. Sometimes they had been ashore for a couple of days before they even went home to their wives. To say they were heavy drinkers was an understatement, they used to drink more than fish.

One of the deckhands who worked on one of the channel boats was a Scottish guy called Murray. He was a typical fisherman, he didn't care how hard he had to work when he was at sea because he knew that when he got back to St Helier he would have a decent wedge in his pocket. It was rare for a deckhand to earn less than a grand for a trip and back in the eighties that was a lot of money. On the run up to Christmas with the price of crab rocketing it was not unusual for their wages to double.

On one trip Murray had a very serious accident whilst working on the deck. From what I was told, the crew had hauled, emptied, baited and stacked a string of about a hundred pots ready for shooting back out to sea. The skipper had given the go-ahead to start shooting the pots back out and they were about a half way through them when Murray was passed the wrong pot. By the time anyone had realized he was holding the wrong pot it was too late and the pot he should have been holding came flying out of the stack and smashed straight into his face.

It was a very serious incident they had on board and they were about forty miles from the nearest port. A mayday was put out on the radio and a French helicopter was sent to the scene. He was airlifted and taken to Cherbourg hospital in Normandy as quickly as possible. He was in hospital there for several weeks whilst they operated on him and rebuilt his face. When he was reasonably fit, arrangements were made for him to be transferred to the hospital in St Helier to finish off his recovery.

Several of us were drinking in the Folie when we heard the news that he was back in Jersey and in the general hospital. He was a popular guy so a bunch of us got into a taxi to pay him a visit and see how he was. Eventually, we found the ward he was in and we were granted permission to visit him. We were shocked when we saw him, his head had bits of metal all around it and there were nuts and bolts everywhere holding it all together. It was almost as if his head had a 'Meccano' cage stuck on it.

Murray was over the moon to see some people he knew after his stay in the French hospital. He was desperate to get out and about for a few hours and we somehow managed to persuade the nurse on duty to let us take him out. She made us swear that the cage on his head would be well protected and she made us promise that he would not drink anything alcoholic. We left the hospital, jumped in a taxi and told him what the nurse had said on our way back to the Folie. As soon as we entered the pub a cheer went up for him and before we could say anything people were buying him drinks. It seemed like everyone wanted to buy him one and within minutes he had given in to the temptation and started.

The drinks were flowing freely and everyone was in high spirits. Someone decided it would be funny to tweak one of the bolts on the cage on his head, and the place erupted with laughter. Someone else tweaked another bolt, and then another bolt was tweaked. Within a short space of time his head started to change shape. It was hilarious and the more tweaks his cage got the more his face altered. The place was in uproar, he looked like something out of a Tom and Jerry cartoon.

Eventually the place settled down and it came to the time when we had to get him back to the hospital. We tried tweaking the bolts to get the cage back to its original position. It only made matters worse and we gave up in the end. We were very concerned, not only had we got him pissed, we had probably undone all the good work that the two hospitals had done between them in repairing his face. We had promised to do two things and we had failed miserably on both accounts. When we arrived at the hospital the senior nurse on duty went mad. She was screaming at us, shouting things like 'You may have damaged him for life' and 'How can anyone be stupid enough to let this happen'. Looking back at it she was right, we could have got the poor bloke permanently brain damaged. Fortunately, Murray made a full recovery and returned to sea later that year to continue fishing.

A trip home with a difference

Just like everyone else, we had our fair share of arguments and experienced plenty of ups and downs. I remember on one occasion having a big fall out with Teresa and she packed her bags and buggered off back to England. It was towards the end of November which meant we had been in Jersey for about eighteen months.

Christmas came and went and there was no sign of her returning. I had been surrounded by both her friends and my own and everyone had made a real effort to make it as good a time as possible during the festivities. I felt pretty down at times and the loneliness really kicked in on the 23rd December when the last ferry had left the island before the Christmas break. I had a young daughter Hayley back in the UK who I hadn't seen for ages and I was really missing my family. To be honest I felt really lonely, no matter how much effort people had put in to making sure I was OK, it had made me realize that real friendships take years to form and being around family is priceless.

Anyway, once Christmas and the New Year celebrations were over I decided to fly home for a few days and catch up with everyone. I arranged for someone to cover me should the boat set to sea whilst I was away although it was unlikely due to the spring tides. I packed my bags, had a couple of beers in the Folie and then caught a bus to the airport. On arrival I bought a ticket to fly to Southampton and checked in. I was pulled over by some customs and excise people who made a thorough search of my bag, before ordering me to strip down to my underwear and going on to examine absolutely everything that was in my possession.

They then went on to interrogate me (that is what it felt like) demanding to know where I was going and why. After being questioned, several phone calls were made. They were making me feel very uneasy, something wasn't quite right, and I couldn't work out what it was. Fortunately, about twenty minutes later they allowed me to proceed with my journey.

I boarded the plane and in less than an hour was back on the ground again in Southampton. I was starting to get excited at the thought of seeing everyone and had completely forgotten about the incident at the airport until I entered the arrivals hall. It was here that I saw a group of people carefully studying everyone that had got off the plane. It was obvious that they were the CID, they stuck out like a sore thumb and to this day I have never met one that looked any different. I could see that they were watching every move that I made so I collected my bags from the conveyor belt and made a quick exit from the airport.

I headed straight to the train station, purchased a ticket and boarded a train to London. Sure enough, I was being followed, they boarded the same train and sat not far away in the same compartment. I decided to have a drink, so I made my way to the buffet car. Two of them followed me, I purchased a couple of cans of beer and then returned to my seat. You've guessed it, back came Bodie and Doyle and sat down with Regan and Carter again. It was crystal clear to me that it was me and nobody else that they were following. As the train got closer to London I made out that I was going to the toilet and jumped off at Clapham Junction instead of waiting till we arrived at Waterloo. It was quite funny really, I gave them a wave from the platform as the train pulled away.

I then found a phone box and called my parents. I had told the customs people that this was where I was going and assumed that this was where the police would go to find me. My dad answered the phone and I let him know what had happened and told him to expect a knock at the door from the police. I told him to just tell them that he had not seen me and assumed I was still on route home. I then telephoned Teresa and arranged for her to pick me up at Birchington station. We hadn't spoken for a while and she had no idea that I was going to be back in the UK. She had made plans with several friends to go to Holland for the weekend on the ferry. Fortunately for me someone had dropped out meaning there was a spare ticket available. Within a few hours of being back in Kent, I found myself on the Isle of Sheppey boarding a ferry to Holland!

We had a great weekend, there was loads of food and drink on board and it just felt great being around long term friends again. We arrived back at Sheerness on the Sunday afternoon and made our way straight to my parent's house in Margate. After the usual hugs and kisses my dad informed me that the police had indeed been round and told him that I was not to return to Jersey without reporting to the police station.

I reluctantly went to the police station where I was advised that a warrant had been issued for my arrest in connection with an unpaid fine for a motoring offence. They let me go on the condition that I went to the courthouse and cleared the outstanding amount before returning to Jersey. Failure to do so would result in me getting arrested at Southampton airport.

I caught up with my daughter and as many other people as I could over the next couple of days and then went to the courthouse to sort everything out before returning to Jersey. Teresa came back with me, and as soon as the plane landed we made our way to the Folie. I then proceeded to phone the bank and I cancelled the cheque that I had written out to clear my fine at the courthouse!

Another trip back home

I got into the regular habit of speaking with my dad every Sunday lunch time. He knew that I would be in the Folie and the phone there would ring dead on twelve o clock. It was such a regular thing that nobody else (even the staff) bothered to answer it because they knew it would be for me.

He had telephoned one evening trying to get hold of me, but unfortunately, I wasn't there, I had already left to go home. The first I knew about the phone call was the following morning whilst I was eating my breakfast in the harbour café. Someone came in and told me that he had rung, he also said there was nothing to worry about and could I ring home as soon as possible. As you do, I immediately thought something serious had happened so went straight to the nearest phone box and called home.

I can't remember if it was mum or dad that answered but I was very relieved to find out that everything was OK. They wanted to let me know that my kid sister was just about to make me an uncle. She had been taken into the hospital the night before and the baby was due anytime now. When they answered the phone to me they actually thought that it would probably be the hospital ringing. I decided to fly home and see my sister so I got a message to Teresa and cancelled work for a couple of days. I went back to the flat and packed a few things into a hold all, scribbled a short note to Teresa confirming I had gone and caught a bus to the airport. On arrival at the airport I found out that the only affordable flight I could get was leaving in an hour for Southampton rather than Gatwick.

I purchased the ticket and by mid-morning I found myself in the arrivals hall at Southampton. My next task was to try and get to Margate with only a few quid in my pocket. I decided that the cheapest way would be to hitch hike. Several people stopped and gave me a lift to various roundabouts and junctions. They varied from van drivers to a driving instructor to a right sexy looking woman who pulled a bloody great machete out from under her seat! She advised me that she was quite happy to give me a lift and quite happy to use it if I tried anything on with her. Unfortunately, although I was grateful, most of the lifts I managed to get were only for a short distance. Eventually, I did make it to the M25.

The first mistake I made on the motorway was to thumb a lift from a police car. He stopped and picked me up and gave me a right bollocking for being on a motorway on foot. I listened carefully as he talked to me and did at least get a lift for about twenty miles from him before he pulled off the motorway and dropped me off. I thanked him and promised him that I would not make the same mistake again. He drove off and I waited a few minutes and then headed back to the hard shoulder to continue my journey. About ten minutes passed and then the same police car came whizzing past me, fortunately he was going in the opposite direction. A lorry sounded his horn and pulled over to pick me up. This time I was in luck because he was heading for the port of Dover which was only about twenty miles from my final destination. He dropped me off just outside Dover and wished me luck with the last leg of the journey. I managed to get a lift and finally arrived in Margate at about half past nine in the evening. I was starving so I grabbed some fish and chips and ate them whilst I walked to the hospital.

I couldn't believe it, when I got there it was all locked up for the night. Back in them days there were strict visiting hours and the only way in to the hospital was via A&E. I decided to walk around the outside of the maternity department and see if I could spot my sister in any of the wards there. I found a ward with a load of incubators in it and sure enough she was in there next to a very small baby that looked like it was in some sort of a fish tank. I tapped on the window to get her attention and she jumped up and opened the window for me to climb in. We were having loads of hugs and kisses when an angry looking matron burst into the room. She started shouting at me and called for help. She looked at me and then she looked at the baby and smiled. In a soft voice she said to me 'You are not supposed to be in here, but my god doesn't he look like you!'

A couple of doctors came running into the ward to see what was wrong and the matron said to them 'It's OK, Tanya's husband is here to see his new son'. It was hilarious, and we let them think it so that we were left in peace. All the staff were congratulating me, I was given tea and biscuits and told I would have to leave before the shift change in the morning. I stayed for about three hours before leaving and making my way to mum and dads house. I stayed in Margate on this occasion for four days and managing to spend quite a bit of time with my daughter Hayley before heading back to Jersey.

I hate Mondays

After several months of thought and deliberation we both decided that it was time to return to England. We had been in Jersey for a good three years and life had seemed to become somewhat claustrophobic. We were both really missing our friends and family back home and for some strange reason the thought of living in Margate and fishing out of Ramsgate harbour really seemed to appeal to me.

We had started out on a small boat, we had progressed to a room and then to two rooms. It was nothing special, but it meant we had a bedroom and a lounge, and we only had to share a bathroom with one other tenant. Due to the acute shortage of property on the island and its location, our accommodation was very sought after. Ricky and Caroline new someone that wanted to move in when we moved out and managed to get someone to give us £250 for the carpets, TV, toaster etc just to get their hands on the door keys. We did a deal and arranged to move out on the following Monday morning. With the money we purchased our airline tickets and bought a few presents to take with us.

I made arrangements to go out on a bender on the Sunday and say my farewells and Teresa did the same. We started at eleven o clock in the Folie and it wasn't long before I knew it was going to get messy. The licencing laws were different from the UK, on a Sunday the pubs were open for two hours from eleven in the morning until one o clock. They then closed until four thirty when they opened again until eleven in the evening. We used to find a restaurant with an alcohol license and eat whilst the pubs were shut and there was plenty to choose from.

Jersey was always joked about as having 78,000 alcoholics clinging to a rock and for the three years that we were there we did our best to make it 78,002. Anyway, having had a session in the Folie and a few more in the restaurant I found myself back where I started. Teresa had gone off with her mates and I was drinking like it was going out of fashion with the fishermen. When the final bell rang I was as pissed as a parrot and the guys I was with were getting concerned about me. They knew that there was no way a taxi would take me home and they knew that I was incapable of walking there.

One of the guys in the pub had a houseboat he was renovating. It was moored up very close to the pub in a tidal part of the harbour. The boat floated for about two hours either side of high water which had been about eight o clock. He suggested that I slept on it but warned me that I would have to be gone shortly after six the next morning. It seemed like the perfect solution to my problem, so I took him up on his offer. I said my farewells to everyone which seemed to take forever and then staggered off across the harbour mud towards his boat. I clambered aboard, took my shoes off and then crawled into a bunk. Within minutes I was fast asleep.

Several hours later I woke up to the sound of lapping water. I opened my eyes to brilliant sunshine and I could hear the seagulls singing outside. I lay there for a few seconds trying to work out where I was and then it hit me. I was on a boat with the tide coming in and I had a plane to catch. I crawled out of the cabin, my head was pounding, I felt sick and to top it all I was scared to fart in case I shit myself. I soon saw that I was marooned, I had overslept, and the tide had come in. Realization set in that I had a major problem on my hands, the clock was against me and I had a plane to catch to the UK with a non-transferable ticket. I was up a creek without a paddle. I desperately searched the boat looking for something to get ashore with but there was nothing. The last place I looked was in a rear compartment and to my amazement there was a tiny dinghy in it. There weren't any oars but that didn't matter, I only had to go about fifty metres to the harbour wall and I could do that using my hands as paddles.

I put my plan into action and gently lowered the dinghy over the side of the boat. I then tied it to the rails and sat down to smoke a fag before putting my shoes on. I had a good look around the harbour for the last time and then decided it was time to go. My hangover had disappeared, and the panic was over. It was a beautiful day and I could see loads of people on the quayside walking their dogs. I carefully climbed over the rail and gently lowered myself into the dinghy. Everything then seemed to turn to slow motion as the dinghy slowly stood on end with me in it and gracefully started to slip under the water.

I couldn't believe what was happening, disaster had struck, my passport, my plane ticket, my wallet, my fags and my lighter were all rapidly heading for the water. To make matters worse, I had attracted a lot of attention from the people on the quay. I was fully clothed and disappearing into the ocean with all my worldly possessions. As the water passed my waist and headed for my neck I looked at my audience and did none other than shout 'I hate Mondays' before letting go of the dinghy and swimming to the shore.

Back in good old Thanet

We arrived back in Thanet and stayed with Teresa's parents at their place in Minster for a couple of weeks whilst we sorted ourselves out. I went back on the boats fishing out of Ramsgate Harbour and Teresa went back into the hairdressing game. At first, she worked in a shop as an employee, and then very quickly she amassed a client base and started working for herself as a mobile hairdresser.

We found a furnished flat that was available to rent in Westgate-on-sea and Teresa made an appointment to sign all the relevant paperwork, pay deposits etc and obtained the keys. Very quickly she was approved to rent the place and we moved in to start a new chapter in our lives. Things were fine for a while, we had a new home and we were both working but then life started to get a bit boring. I am not sure quite what caused it, it could have been the fact that we were living in Thanet again, it could have been the reduction in income I had to contend with (I was certainly earning a lot more working in Jersey) or it could have just been the fact that life was becoming far too routine.

The inevitable happened and we went our separate ways. I moved out of the flat and moved in with my sister and her boyfriend where they lived in Cliftonville. Things were fine staying there with them and it was only ever going to be a temporary thing. The flat they had was above a greengrocer's and there was never any shortage of fresh vegetables to eat. I made sure there was plenty of fresh fish or crab to go with the veg and all in all we ate very well indeed. Several weeks into staying with my sister I got the urge to patch things up with Teresa and decided to go over and see her. It wasn't a matter of grabbing my mobile phone and ringing her, they hadn't been invented back then. The only way to see her was to jump on a bus and physically call at her address in person.

I showered and changed and then caught the bus to Westgate. I jumped off at the station bus stop and made my way to the flat. I was gutted when I got there to find out she wasn't even in. I didn't have a key to open the door, so I decided to break the lock and gain access this way. The flat door was inside the main building and up a flight and a half of stairs, so it would not cause anyone in the street to be alarmed with my actions. Once in I could make myself a cup of tea, put my feet up and simply wait for her to return.

I put my shoulder to the door and the woodwork around the lock split easily. I entered the flat and headed straight for the kitchen to put the kettle on. I could only have been there for a couple of minutes when three bloody great coppers came charging in and grabbed me. Before I could say anything I had pinned been to the floor. They handcuffed me with my arms behind my back, they read me the riot act and then they frog marched me out of the building. I frantically tried to tell them that they were making a mistake and that I lived there but they were having none of it.

They chucked me in the back of the police car, and one of them sat next to me and before I knew it. I was in front of the custody officer at Margate Police station. I tried explaining to him that a mistake had been made and that I lived there and had only broke the door because I had lost my keys. He was having none of it either and I ended up in the cells. I was advised that as soon as Teresa could be located to verify my story I would be free to go but until such time I would be kept behind bars with the possibility of being charged with criminal damage and attempted burglary. I asked several times if they had found her to which they had replied that they hadn't. It was getting beyond a joke and time was getting on now, it was well after ten o clock in the evening. I told them that they would be able to find her in a nightclub up the road called the Caprice and asked them to please send someone there to see her so that I could be let out.

They agreed to send someone round there to see if they could find her. About three quarters of an hour later the copper came back from the nightclub. He had a horrible sort of a smile on his face, he looked at me and then said, 'You were right mate, she is in there and you might as well make yourself comfortable because she says that she has no idea at all of who you are'. I spent the whole night in the cells pacing up and down and thinking to myself what a bitch she could be at times.

Another brush with the old bill

I soon got fed up with having to catch the bus every time I needed to get to somewhere. Whether it be the harbour or the pub or the fishmongers it was a pain in the arse so I looked around for a cheap car. I located a mustard coloured Austin Maxi which was for sale at the right price. It was just what I needed, it had three seats in the back that folded away to make a massive boot space. It was one of the first cars designed with a hatchback and it meant that I could carry several boxes of fish if I needed to. It was taxed, it was MOT'd, and most importantly it was legal so I bought it. Parking was not a problem, there was a big public carpark to the rear of my sister's place and you only had to pay to park there during the day. It suited me just fine, during the day the car was parked on the harbour wall and at night when it was free it was in the carpark.

Life became so much easier with some wheels to get around in until I came home one day to find it had gone. Someone had nicked it, I checked everywhere, I knew where I had left it but started doubting myself. I checked the harbour to no avail, I checked the pub, I even asked my sister who couldn't even drive if she had used it. It was nowhere to be found and I had no choice in the end other than to notify the insurance company that it had been stolen and report the matter to the police. Things then went from bad to worse, it turned out that my sister's boyfriend Nigel had 'borrowed' it without asking me and gone to Broadstairs in it to pick up some weed. The police had spotted the car and signalled him to stop. He was having none of it, especially with a bag of weed in his pocket. He hit the accelerator and drove off like a lunatic as fast as he could. The police gave chase and eventually after about twenty minutes of being on the run Nigel had realized that he was not going to get away from them and pulled over.

He was arrested, read his rights and then he was escorted to the police station. Inside the station Nigel was questioned about the car and a statement was taken from him. In his statement he advised them that I had told him that he had permission to use the car whenever he wanted to. He was then released pending further enquiries into the matter. The police called around to my sisters to see me, I was not home so they left a message with her asking me to report to the police station as soon as I could as a matter of urgency. Fortunately, Nigel was home when I got in and he was able to tell me everything that had happened. He was also able to tell me exactly what he had said to them. I had no idea what I was going to say to them or how we were going to get out of the mess we were in but at least I was aware of the situation.

I reported to the police station as requested and was asked to take a seat in the waiting room whilst they found the officer that was dealing with the case. He turned up after about ten minutes and ushered me through the reception area and into an interview room. I was asked if I knew Nigel to which I told them I did. I was then asked if I had let him borrow the car to which I told them I had. At this point things started to get a bit tricky, the policeman was adamant that he was going to get a prosecution and I was given one of two choices. The first choice was that Nigel would be charged with theft of a motor vehicle and that was subject to me sticking to my original statement in court. If I refused to agree to do that and I withdrew my statement, the second choice was going to be that I was going to be the one that was charged. They were going to charge me with wasting police time.

I was in shit street, what the fuck was I going to do. I could either get my sister's boyfriend nicked or I could get myself nicked. I didn't want to cause my sister any grief, after all she had been good enough to put me up in her flat and Nigel was a nice guy, he had just been a bit stupid in taking the car without asking if it was OK. I took a chance and said to the copper 'I am not someone who would shit on family just so that you can convict someone, so you will have to prosecute me'

It turned out that they had no intention of charging me, they were hoping to frighten me into sticking with my story. He had been after charging Nigel for a couple of things that had happened in the past and had seen this as a way of getting him into court. Fortunately for both of us, nobody was charged and we both ended up with just a good old verbal warning regarding the matter.

Bad Taste Party

I ended up patching things up with Teresa and we decided to buy a house together in Cliftonville. We were only there for about eight months and it became pretty apparent to both of us that it wasn't going to work out. We came up with a solution over the house and the finances and I ended up buying her out. With the money that she got back out of the house in Cliftonville she managed to buy another property in Garlinge which was about three miles away. Fortunately, it was a very amicable split up and we remained good friends still socializing with the same circles of people and even at the same times on a few occasions.

I had been seeing a girl called Debi who became the mother of my second daughter Rowanne, and within a relatively short space of time she had vacated her flat and moved into my house. Everything was fine, there was no bad feelings from Teresa, in fact she seemed to be quite pleased for me. Even though I had lived in the house for quite a while Debi was insistent on having a house warming party. I kept saying that there was no point and I reminded her on several occasions that she might have just moved in to the house but I hadn't. In the end it was easier to just agree with her and to start making a list of who to invite.

We discussed the party over the next few days and decided that we would make it a 'bad taste party'. In other words, people were to turn up in awful clothing that didn't match or didn't fit or was about thirty years out of date. The invites went out to both of our families, my work mates, her friends and my circle of friends. The response was unbelievable, it seemed that virtually everyone we knew had accepted the invitation and to add to the fun they all said they would be dressing up. The only person that was invited that declined the offer was Teresa, she just said that she wouldn't feel right going to a party in her old house with the situation as it was. There wasn't much I could do or say other than something to the effect of 'if you change your mind you know where we are, and you are more than welcome'

I arranged to borrow a decent sound system for the evening and we purchased huge amounts of alcohol from the supermarket. I then set about trying to find a decent outfit to wear. I couldn't find anything suitable anywhere and time was running out fast. In the end I came up with a plan which would entail making my outfit. I went through my cloths and found a white shirt and a coloured shirt, some black trousers and some coloured trousers. I then found two pairs of shoes that were different colours and a pair of odd socks. Next was a pair of scissors and all the clothes were cut in half from top to bottom. I then put the left side of the clothing that I had sorted out with the right side of the clothing that was a different colour and stitched them back together.

It worked well, if I stood right side facing the mirror you couldn't see that the left side was completely different and visa versa. The only problem I had was my face and hair looked the same from both sides. I telephoned Teresa and explained the situation and asked if she could cut my hair. She agreed to do it and I arranged to call round on the Saturday morning of the party to get it sorted. As per our arrangements I called round to Teresa's house. We had a few drinks and then she set about sorting my hair out. She shaved off the left side of my beard, she shaved off the left side of my moustache and then to finish it off she shaved off the left side of my hair. My hair was quite long at the time and to see the two different images of myself in the mirror was hilarious. She took a photo and wished me good luck with the party. Before I left her place we agreed that I would call around the next morning at about half past eleven to sort my hair out before the pubs opened at twelve o clock.

The party was a total success, my outfit complete with the hair and beard missing from one side of my face meant that I had to have a left and right photo with everyone. People wore all sorts of outrageous stuff with bad taste being the definite theme. I have no idea what time the party ended but it was later than four o clock in the morning. I went to bed and crashed for a few hours and then got up about nine thirty to tidy up a bit before heading round to Teresa's.

I arrived at Teresa's house about ten minutes early and was surprised to find that her car was nowhere to be seen. It was strange because in them days you drove home regardless of how much drink you had. Her front door was on the side of the house and I could see what looked like a note pinned on it. I immediately thought that she might have nipped out to the shop to get some milk or something like that, so I got out of my car and walked up to the front door to read it.

Sure enough, it was a note and it was addressed to me. I couldn't believe it when I read it, all it said was 'Ha ha have a great day'! What a bitch, she had tucked me up again. I felt a right twat, I had arranged to meet everyone for a lunchtime session and here I was with half a haircut and half a beard. In the end I had no choice other than to see the funny side of the situation and go out like it. On arrival at the pub everyone thought it was hilarious and it seemed like some of them already knew that Teresa would not be in.

This isn't fair game

We lived for several years in the house in Cliftonville. The three of us, me Debi and Rowanne became four when Debi's dad Terry fell out with his girlfriend and moved in. He became a mate rather than a father-in-law and he was often my passport to getting out of the house for a few beers. When Rowanne was just over two years old Lauren came along to make our family complete.

I can still remember the night Lauren was born, I had been out for a few beers and had got home at around midnight. Debi's sister Hayley was staying over and the first thing she said to me when I walked through the door was 'Debi has gone into labour you have got to take her to the hospital straight away.' I didn't take much notice of her at first, the baby wasn't due for at least another week. I soon realized that Hayley was being serious when I heard Debi taking deep breaths and having contractions. I quickly grabbed the keys to Terry's pick up, helped her get into the passenger seat and then shot off towards the hospital. Thankfully the hospital wasn't very far away because there was no way I should have been driving. I was probably at least four times the drink drive limit.

We arrived safely at the hospital and promptly had an argument over who needed to sit in the wheelchair. Was it to be Debi because she was having contractions and about to give birth at any minute or was it to be me because I had had a skin full and could hardly walk. In the end the nurses decided on two wheelchairs and we were both wheeled down to the Labour suite. I sobered up rapidly with everything that was going on and a few hours later Lauren successfully entered the world. I stayed there for a couple of hours and then when I was sure that everything was OK left the hospital to give everyone the good news. The next day Debi was able to leave the hospital and come home complete with our new baby.

A week or so later I went out with Terry for a few celebration drinks. We knew that it would end up being a heavy session so bearing this in mind we deliberately left the vehicles behind. This way neither of us would be tempted to drive our cars home and they would be there to use in the morning. We managed to get home by about midnight, I went straight to bed with my alarm set for 5am to get up for work. It felt like I had only just shut my eyes when the alarm started ringing and it was time to get up. I jumped out of bed, stuck some clothes on and grabbed a cup of tea before heading off to the harbour. I had only driven about a mile when I spotted a police car with blue flashing lights behind me. I pulled over to let him past. To my dismay he didn't pass, he pulled over as well. He got out of his car and walked over to me. I wound my window down to speak to him and the first thing he asked was had I been drinking. I laughed and said to him 'You are joking aren't you I have just got up and I am on my way to work.'

He was having none of it, he stuck his head in the car and told me that he could smell alcohol and that he was going to breathalyse me. He was very smug, it seemed like he was desperate to nick someone and his actual words to me were 'If the light on this thing turns red you are in the shit'. Sure enough, after about thirty seconds of blowing into it the light turned red. They arrested me and carted me off to the police station.

On arrival there I found that it was a female police officer in charge. I pleaded with her that this was not fair game. I explained that I had recently become a dad again and had been out to celebrate the birth with my father-in-law. I even told her that I had not taken the car out with me because I hated people that drove whilst over the limit. I said to her that if I had been deliberately drink driving I would have been a fair cop but that it was very unfair to try and nick a bloke on his way to work the next day. She seemed to agree with what I had said but advised me that she could not let me go without testing me again for drink driving because I had been arrested on suspicion of it.

She went on to explain the procedure to me, I was to take two tests on this bloody great thing on the wall and they had to be twenty minutes apart. She advised me that the limit was 35ml for drink driving and that they would act on the lowest of the two readings taken. After confirming to her that I understood everything I was given the first test. I blew into the machine and then waited. It seemed to take forever and then it flashed and stopped dead on 35ml. She looked at me with a big smile on her face and said 'You will be pleased to know that you will be free to go after your second test in twenty minutes time and you will not be charged for drink driving as the reading is on the limit and not over it'

Sure enough, twenty minutes later I took the test again and she advised me that I could leave. She then asked me if I had any questions or if she could help me in any way. I thought for a minute and then asked her 'is there any chance you can get me a lift to the harbour before I miss the morning tide?' No problem was her reply and she instructed the two coppers that had tried to nick me to drop me over to Ramsgate harbour.

In the police car one of the coppers turned around and said to me 'I bet you didn't think you would get away with that did you?' I just sat there looking at him and replied with 'No I didn't, and I bet you thought that you would have clocked off by now and was on your way home now rather than driving me to Ramsgate'. The rest of the journey was completed in silence.

Running a business from home

In addition to using nets to catch fish, we used to use pots to catch whelks as well. They certainly weren't the most exciting thing in the sea to catch but they did prove to be good when it came to providing us with a steady income, and just to put the icing on the cake, it didn't cost much to get set up if you were prepared to put some effort in.

I used to make my own whelk pots, I won't bore you with the finer details of how they were made but it was something along these lines. I would get hold of a load of five gallon (25 litre) plastic containers. I would unscrew the lids and give them a quick wash out with the garden hose to remove any chemicals or liquid that they had been used to supply and then screw the lids firmly back on. The containers would then all be laid down on their side so that they were all facing the same way. With an electric drill and a jigsaw I would cut a hole in the side about the size of a large side plate. Once this was done, I would turn the containers over so that the side with the cut out was facing the ground and I would hammer a 6in nail into the opposite side. Once this was done the containers were turned back over and about two inches of concrete was poured into each one and left to settle around the nail.

They were left to set for at least 48 hours and then I drilled loads of holes in the rest of the container so that they would fill up with water and sink down onto the seabed. To finish the pot off a piece of netting was put around the entrance (the big hole I had cut out) to prevent the whelks from getting out once they were in the pot. These pots were now ready to fish, all I had to do was load them onto the boat and connect them all to a backline. This being a rope with each pot tied on to it by its handle about every 15 yards. Finally, a lump of dogfish was stuck on the nail in each pot as bait and they were ready to go.

One day there was a knock at my front door. I opened it and there was a bloke standing there with an identification badge in his hand. He explained to me that he was from Thanet District Council and had been asked to call at my house following a complaint they had received from a neighbour. Apparently, I had been reported for storing large quantities of dangerous chemicals in my back garden. I invited him in and took him through the house and out into the garden. I pointed to this neat pile of 25ltr drums and said something to the effect of 'I expect it is these that are causing the problem'. With that I walked up to them and picked one up. I took the top off and turned it upside down to empty it. He was surprised to find out that they were all empty. I then took the trouble to tell him that I was a commercial fisherman and I explained exactly what the containers were for and how I made them into whelk pots. He apologised for any inconvenience caused by his visit and thanked me for my help in resolving the issue and left to report his findings back to the council. I had a pretty good idea about who had put the complaint in and quickly forgot about the visit. It didn't matter anyway as I had resolved the issue.

About two weeks passed by when I had another knock on my door. I answered the door to be greeted by someone from the council again, the only difference being that this guy held a much higher position there. He introduced himself and told me that the reason for his visit was because he had heard reports that I was operating a business from a residential property without council permission. I flatly denied the allegation and he asked me if he could come in and could we go out into the back garden. I agreed and let him in. He made a beeline for the backdoor and headed straight out into the garden and over to my pile of containers. He picked one up and accused me of turning them into whelk pots. He explained exactly what had to be done from the cutting of the first hole in the drum to the nails that were used to the concrete that was poured into them. He even explained how they were tied together in strings of twenty and baited up with dogfish on the nail before being shot at sea. He had basically repeated word for word what I had told his colleague on the earlier visit.

I looked him up and down and then said to him 'I am sorry to disappoint you, but I do not make these so called whelk pots out of them. If you really want to know what I do with them I will tell you. I cut the whole of one side out of the container and lay it on its side. I half fill it up with compost and carefully plant a couple of tomato plants in it. I grow the tomato plants in these containers rather than straight in the ground because the slugs can't get into them. This enables me to have fresh sliced home grown tomato's with mature cheddar cheese on my sandwiches. I think that the best thing that you can do is fuck off out of my sight and don't come back again.'

With that I showed him the way to the front door.

How do you keep a straight face?

As the kids started to grow up they both ended up having a favourite parent. I don't know why because they were both treated the same, but Rowanne was always a mummies girl and Lauren was completely the opposite, she was a daddy's girl. They both went to the same junior school (Cliftonville Primary) which was only about a half a mile from the house. It was usually Debi, but which ever one of us took them or picked them up from school the easiest way was to walk. Driving there was OK but it was an absolute pain in the arse trying to find somewhere to park.

I was working on the boat one day and Debi was tasked with picking the girls up. On arrival at the school Laurens teacher made a bee line for her and she was summonsed into the classroom. The teacher then went on to explain to her that Lauren had been swearing and using some choice words in the playground. She was in her first year at school at the time, she would only have been about five years old, and this was not acceptable. Something had to be done to put a stop to it.

I arrived home from the boat a couple of hours later totally unaware of what had occurred at the school earlier with Lauren. It was the norm for me to open the front door and have Lauren charging full belt towards me and almost knocking me over. On this particular day she didn't run to me, in fact she was nowhere to be seen. This seemed very odd to me, I walked through to the kitchen where Debi was cooking the dinner and asked her where Lauren was. I could see Rowanne playing in the back garden and she was clearly out there on her own.

She told me that she had had a very embarrassing meeting with the teacher when she arrived to pick the girls up from school. She then went on to tell me about Lauren and the bad language she had been using. As a result, Debi had sent her to her bedroom. I made myself a cup of tea and then went upstairs to get my dirty fishing gear off and run a bath. As I passed Lauren's bedroom I opened the door to let her know that I was home, and also to let her know that it was totally unacceptable for her to be using foul language.

As I poked my head into her room I could see Lauren sitting on the bed having total hysterics. Her laughter was uncontrollable, I didn't know what it could be, but she had certainly found something funny. I remember thinking to myself that if this was punishment for her use of swear words it wasn't working. I looked at her with a stern face and said something to the effect of 'Come on then, what are you finding so funny? You have been sent to your room for being naughty, and this is no laughing matter.' It took her a couple of minutes, to stop laughing and then she managed to blurt out the following, 'Mum has washed my mouth out with a bar of soap and I can still say fuck!

Lost in France

Money always seemed to be tight when the kids were young, but we managed to somehow give them at least one family holiday every year. My parents had a cottage in a place called Mauron, it was in Brittany in the north west of France and at the time they were still living in the United Kingdom. It was the obvious place to go, we only had to pay for a ferry ticket and fuel for the car to be able to take the kids on holiday.

I always booked the ferry for the last week of the summer holidays going into the first three days of when the schools re-opened. I would rather of not kept the kids off school but doing it this way made the ferry ticket so much cheaper. I had a few heated words with Hayley's mum one year over the dates I had booked. Eventually she backed down and agreed that Hayley could come with us. This was great, it meant that I could have a holiday with all my three children at the same time.

When the dates came around to depart we loaded the car up and I mean loaded it. We set off for France with five people in the car, that being two adults in the front and the three kids in the back. On top of that, we had a roof box that was crammed to the absolute maximum with holiday clothing and food and a bike rack on the back of the car with three pushbikes strapped to it. We had a pleasant ferry crossing from Portsmouth to St Malo and we booked an overnight cabin so that the children could get some sleep. In later years this route became far too expensive and time consuming, so we switched to the Dover Calais route followed by a long drive on the other side. We docked in St Malo on this occasion and just over an hour later we were safely parked up at my mum and dads house. The kids went for a bit of a wander whilst we switched the electric and water on and unloaded the car. Our clothing was put away, the bikes were taken off the rack and extra beds were made up for the three of them. We made a list of what stuff we needed from the supermarket and I went with Hayley to get it whilst Debi sorted out some lunch for everyone.

About three days into the holiday Hayley decided to go off on a bike ride on her own. Rowanne and Lauren went off after her and we never really gave it a thought to check up on them. It is so remote where my parents house is you might only see one or two cars all day long so the roads were really safe. About an hour or so later Hayley returned on her own. We asked about the other two and she told us that she had gone off on her own right from the first bend in the road. Now it was time to get worried, as far as Hayley was concerned, she had shot off on her own thinking that the other two would turn back and they hadn't arrived. I jumped in the car with Hayley and we went to look for them. Debi stayed behind so that someone was at the house if they came back whilst we were looking.

We searched everywhere, stopping at every junction and getting out and calling them. It was no good, they were nowhere to be seen and to make matters worse the light was starting to fade. I went back to the house in the hope of finding them there. They weren't there, I was starting to feel sick, something terrible must have happened, someone must have abducted them or something.

Fortunately, although it was only a summer home, my parents had a telephone there and the line was active. I frantically searched for a number for the police station to get help, praying that when I got through there would be someone there that spoke English. Miraculously, before I could find the number the phone rang. I answered it and someone who could speak very little English asked for Mr Barratt (my dad). It turned out he was ringing from a village that was about six miles away and was looking for my dad because his wife had found two English children that were clearly lost. He hadn't expected the kids to be anything to do with us, he had only rung up so that an English person could speak to them and find out what was wrong and where they lived. They had invited the children into their house whilst they tried to sort things out and the kids had refused to go. We had always drilled it into them that they were never to go off with strangers, ironically, on this occasion they would have been safe to do so.

The relief of knowing they were OK was unbelievable, I think we all had tears running down our faces. I wrote down the address and went to collect them straight away. I couldn't thank these wonderful people enough for what they had done. We all returned there the next day with a thank you card and flowers. Over the years we had loads of family holidays in France and it became the norm to put a tape in the cassette player in the car and play Bonnie Tyler's 'Lost in France'.

A student for a day

My daughter Hayley moved to Birmingham to live when she was in her teens. It was sad to see her go but the education standards were much higher in the Midlands than they were in Kent, so it was only right that they went without any objections from me. I had regular telephone contact with her and drove to Birmingham to see her three or four times a year. I always went on a weekend and very often Lauren came with me which was great both for me on the journey and for the two sisters to see each other. We would usually go to somewhere like TFI Fridays to eat or go rock climbing in an old converted warehouse.

I remember going to visit her on my own on one occasion. Hayley by this time was studying at Birmingham University and had moved out of her mother's house. She was living in digs with four other girls and invited me up to stay for the weekend. It seemed like a good idea and I agreed. It was soon established that all I needed for the weekend was a change of clothes my wash gear and a sleeping bag. The weekend soon arrived and with written instructions (it was before the days of satellite navigation) I set off for her address. It was a good trip there and the house was easy to find. On arrival I was gasping for a cup of tea, I made myself at home and stuck the kettle on. I went to the fridge to find there was no milk, in fact there was absolutely nothing in the fridge, it was so empty they may as well have turned it off and saved the electric.

I found out after chatting to Hayley and the four girls she was sharing the house with that food shopping was very low on the priority list. In fact, it didn't even make the list at all! Hayley had the answer to my tea requirements, she wanted to show me where she went to University and the canteen would be open. Not only could I get a cup of tea it was cheap and cheerful to eat there. The two of us went off leaving her housemates behind to make our way to the Uni. Fortunately, it was only around the corner and before I knew it we were in the canteen. As we entered Hayley nudged me and said something like 'Don't forget you are a student, its 20 percent cheaper!' We ordered drinks and a meal and after about ten minutes of banter with the girl on the till I managed to get the discount by convincing her that I was studying as a mature student.

We ate and caught up on everything that had happened since the last conversation we had had and then left to make our way back to the house. I asked her what was planned for the night to be told that New Street was the place to be for a bit of life and entertainment. I was up for that and told Hayley to invite her mates along with us as well.

Sure enough, by seven thirty we were all changed, clean and out of the door on our way out. We, that being myself and five giggling female students. At the first pub I got the drinks in for everyone and soon after that we were on the move. I knew that Hayley was probably skint and suspected the others would be as well. It seemed only fair that I treated the other girls like I treated Hayley so without question I paid for all the drinks all evening. We visited several pubs before ending up in a gay bar where we had an absolute blast. The atmosphere was great, the jokes were flying, the drinks were going down well and there was not a hint of any trouble anywhere to be seen. We partied there until the early hours before making our way back to the house.

Once back at the house we all went off to our rooms and before long I was fast asleep. I woke up in the morning to the sound of laughter from the kitchen and I heard one of the girls saying to Hayley 'I wish my dad was like yours'. I glanced in my wallet at the fifteen quid I had left out of two hundred and fifty and thought to myself 'I bet you bloody do!' Taking everything into account it was a great weekend and worth every penny.

Neil

When Rowanne was about twelve years old and Lauren was about ten we were living in a nice four bedroomed house in a place called Westbrook. At the time Debi was the main bread winner and I stayed at home to look after the kids. This was fine by me, it gave me the chance to see my kids grow up and not miss out on such things as school sports days and after school activities.

We decided to become foster parents, it was the perfect way to enable me to carry on bringing the kids up without having to go to work whilst at the same time it would give me mine own income. We had numerous discussions with the girls prior to training and qualifying for this role and everyone agreed that this was a good idea and wouldn't disrupt family life as we knew it. We qualified as a foster family and we were offered several children, unfortunately none of them seemed to fit the bill. We had to have a child that we thought we could help in life and it had to be a child that we thought would fit into our family as one of us. Eventually, we were given details of a lad called Neil that was five years old. We immediately knew that he was the one and within days he was living with us.

Prior to his arriving, we had booked a family holiday to Ibiza for two weeks which we were due to go on a fortnight later. There was no way we were going to have him move in for a couple of weeks and then palm him off whilst we went away. Somehow, I don't really know how we managed to wangle it we got his social workers and his family to agree to him coming abroad with us. We managed to get him booked on the flight and with only two days to spare we succeeded in getting him his passport.

We set off on our holiday arriving at our apartment about lunchtime. We quickly unpacked our bags and set off to check out the swimming pool and whatever other facilities were close to hand. It was great, just below our apartment was a row of restaurants and a convenience store and opposite was a hotel with evening entertainment. To top it all, it was less than a five minute stroll down to a small harbour and a lovely sandy beach. Having checked everything out we relaxed by the pool for a few hours. We decided that we would eat in one of the restaurants on the complex that evening so that we would be able to get the kids to bed early. It had been a long day and although they weren't showing it, we knew they would be tired after such a long day and all the travelling.

Half way through our meal a nightmare started to unfold, we suddenly realized that Neil was missing. One minute he was there and the next minute he had gone. I checked the toilets and he was nowhere to be seen. We asked the people on the next table if they had seen him to no avail. We asked the waiting staff and they hadn't seen him either. We checked outside, still there was no Neil, he had somehow vanished. This was serious, it was certainly no laughing matter. We had taken this young lad, a child that was in care abroad and lost him! I started feeling sick, I was fearing the worse and went off to check the swimming pool. I had visions of finding him floating upside down lifeless. Thankfully he wasn't there, so I returned to the restaurant. By now Debi had raised the alarm and every one that was in the restaurant was frantically searching for him. I walked off towards the beach, I couldn't imagine him going there but I didn't know where else to look. He wasn't there either, so I returned to the restaurant. There was quite a crowd outside by now and everyone was getting really concerned. Neil was nowhere to be found, people had searched everywhere for him, he had simply disappeared. Our holiday had turned into a catastrophe, someone must have abducted him. I asked the restaurant staff to telephone the police and notify them that we had a missing child and needed their help immediately to find him. The manager was fully aware of the situation and had already done so and a few minutes later a police car pulled up. They started asking questions as to what the problem was, what he looked like and when did we realize that Neil was missing, and how did we let him walk out of the restaurant alone!

Suddenly he appeared looking very pleased with himself, and he went on to tell the police how he had hidden himself behind the curtains and how none of these adults had been unable to find him. I didn't know whether to laugh or cry, talk about a relief. I think social services might have had something to say about it, but I have got to admit that at the time I could quite easily have throttled him.

Bob the swimmer

So many funny things happened at Ramsgate Harbour that it has quite rightly earned a section of its own. Some of the things that happened are mentioned in the following pages and they are not necessarily written in any particular order.

We were at sea one day when it suddenly occurred to me to play a prank on a fellow fisherman. It was at the time that mobile phones had just been invented. I had one fitted on the boat at huge expense, it was called a mobile phone, but you had to have a bloody rucksack just to carry the battery it needed to work. The phone that I had was a top of the range Motorola and it worked and looked just like a house phone with a curly cable connecting the receiver to the telephone itself.

Our gear was in the water fishing and we had about three hours to kill before hauling it back. I beckoned to John and Jimmy the two guys that were fishing with me to come over to the wheelhouse. I then told them to be quiet whilst I phoned Richard, he was a great friend of ours that sadly lost his life a few years later. Not only was Richard a commercial fisherman, he was licensed to pilot cross channel swimmers across the channel to France or visa-versa. This was a laborious and boring task but as far as I am aware the money was very good, and no-one could attempt the swim without a support boat to guide them.

Anyway, I telephoned Richard one day (he would have had no idea who I was because the phones did not supply caller details back in them days). He answered the phone and in a serious voice I asked to speak to a Richard Armstrong. He confirmed that he was indeed who I was looking for and then the conversation went something along these lines. 'Good afternoon Sir, I have been given your telephone number by the British Swimming Association. They have advised me that you are the guy to speak to with regards to an attempt at swimming across the English Channel. Is that correct?'

He confirmed that he was the guy I needed to speak to, so I went on to tell him that I wanted to provisionally book a couple of dates for an attempt at the crossing so that in the event of bad weather stopping the first attempt we would have another date to fall back on.' He agreed with me that this was a wise thing to do and asked me to hold on the line whilst he got his diary out. By this time the three of us on board were laughing and sniggering to ourselves, it was obvious to us that he had not only taken the bait, he had taken the hook line and sinker as well. I was really struggling not to laugh out loud, the others thought it was funny as well and they didn't even know what was to follow.

Richard came back on the phone, he thanked me for waiting and then he went on to offer me several dates when his boat was available. He then went through the dates with the local tide table in front of him and advised me of what dates were most favourable to attempt the swim. We agreed on a couple of dates and then I said to him 'Richard, I am not the guy who is going to swim the channel I am his coach'. He advised me that this was normal procedure (I already knew this and just wanted it to sound as genuine as possible) and went on to ask me for the details of the swimmer who was going to attempt to swim the Channel.

'Hopefully, it will not be a problem with insurance or anything like that, I said to him, but the swimmer unfortunately is disabled.' Richard confirmed that this was not a problem and he advised me that he had escorted disabled swimmers across the channel on several occasions. He asked me what the disabilities were so that they could be catered for.

By now I was lying on the deck of the boat, my stomach was really hurting me where I was trying not to laugh. To this day I do not know how I managed to say it without laughing but somehow, I managed to blurt out 'He has no arms or legs and his name is Bob'

I had to put my hand over the receiver, all three of us had lost it completely. It was probably only about half a minute, but it certainly seemed to be a lot longer than that when Richard replied to my comment. All I heard him say was 'Barratt you are a cunt' and with that he hung up.

Muffin the mule

Sticking with Richard for the next story, I was at sea one day and the telephone rang. I answered it and Richard asked me if I knew where he kept his keep pot at sea. A keep pot (for anyone that does not know) is something that you store crabs and lobsters in until they are needed for the market.

I confirmed that I did know the exact whereabouts of it to which he said 'Great, can you take a hundred quid's worth of lobsters out of it and I will meet you at the Mad Chef's Bistro when you have finished.' It turned out that he planned to sell them to Paul and that was what was going to settle our bar tab for the evening.'

At the time, we had a small teddy bear mascot on the dashboard of the boat. I got an elastic band and wrapped it around the hands of the teddy bear as if it was a lobster. It looked quite funny and having lifted his keep pot out of the water and removed the required number of lobsters out of it we put the teddy in with the remaining lobsters. We then steamed back to the harbour unloaded our catch and tied the boat up for the night. We rushed to the merchants to weigh up our catch and then headed down to the Mad Chef's armed with Richards lobsters.

On arrival at the Bistro Richard and his crew Golly were already on the beer with Paul. It wasn't long before I had taken the lobsters downstairs to the kitchen and we had joined them. I have no idea what time we rolled out of Paul's place, but it was very late, and we were certainly well oiled.

Nobody gave the fact that we had been drinking a second thought, we all jumped in our respective vehicles and drove home. It wasn't a problem back in them days, everybody did it. Drinking and driving was the norm. I only had a few miles to go so within a few minutes I would be home. Richard wasn't bothered about being intoxicated and behind the wheel either and he lived over twenty miles away in Deal.

The next day on our way out to sea I was laughing with John my crew mate about the fun we had had the previous evening. We tried to work out when Richard would lift his keep pot and find the banded teddy bear. We gave up in the end, because we had no idea when he would be lobstering again. We would find out soon enough. A couple of days went by and we had heard absolutely nothing. Something wasn't right, their keep pot must have been emptied by now. Our VHF radio crackled, and we heard the name of our boat being called. It was Golly and he was asking us if we had done our lobster pots that morning. I told him we hadn't but were planning to do them this afternoon before we return to the harbour'

I then asked him why he wanted to know and all I got was some feeble response saying something along the lines of 'oh we were just wondering'. I immediately knew they had done something and John agreed with me. We tried to work out what they could have done and came up with the conclusion that they must have tied two strings of pots together. That afternoon we went to clear the pots. We picked up the southern end and proceeded to haul them knowing that something out of the ordinary was going to happen. In came the first pot with no problem, followed by the second and then the third and all the way along the string. I was baffled and getting confused by now, they must have done something to them.

Finally, we came to the last pot. We hauled it aboard, looked inside it and then we looked at each other and burst out laughing. They had wedged a horse's skull inside it and written on the cheekbone with an indelible marker pen was the following message. 'Muffin the mule is an offence!' We had no idea how they managed to get it into the pot because after about twenty minutes of trying to prise it out we gave up and cut a hole in the mesh to remove it.

More fish than we expected

At certain times of the year herring frequent our coastline. They are an easy fish to catch, they taste good, but unfortunately, they are not the easiest things in the world to sell. In an ideal world you would put your nets in the water, let them drift for about a mile and then haul them back with about four or five boxes of fish in them. This would make for easy work and this amount of fish could easily be sold for around thirty quid a box. Any more than five boxes and the price would drop with the usual excuse, that being 'sorry lads there is a glut and we just can't sell them all.'

Anyway, we left the harbour early one evening with our herring gear on board. The plan was simple, we would cast our nets just outside the harbour entrance and let them drift towards Broadstairs. When they had reached Broadstairs we would lift one end and try and assess how many fish we had caught. If it looked like we had caught enough herrings we would haul the gear back and if it looked sparse we would leave them to drift further along the coast.

We shot the gear and marked both ends with a flashing light. It was then that had a brainwave, I looked at the other two crew and with a grin on my face said to them 'Anyone fancy a beer in Broadstairs while the gear makes its way along the coast?' Obviously, I got the response I expected so I radioed port control and made up some feeble excuse that the engine was running a bit hot, so I was heading into Broadstairs harbour to pick up some fresh water. I then asked them to warn any vessels passing by that our gear was in the water and had been left there unattended. Once they confirmed that they would warn anyone about the gear we shot off to have a couple of beers in the Tarter Frigate.

Unfortunately, when we arrived at the Frigate there were a few fishermen there and the couple of beers that we planned turned into a couple of hours. None of us wanted to leave the pub but we knew we had to go and retrieve our gear. We reluctantly said our farewells and left. We put to sea and started to search for the nets. They were nowhere to be seen, they had literally disappeared. I calculated that because of the length of time the gear had been in the water that they would have drifted past Broadstairs and continued on a track to the north so that is the way we headed. A mile past by and still there was no sign of the gear, another mile past and then one of the lads thought he could see a faint flashing light in the distance. I followed his directions and we found the gear wrapped around the longnose buoy!

We started to haul the gear and within minutes we knew that we had a problem. I had never seen so many herrings in my life. We rearranged the boat to try and spread the load. They just kept coming and the boat was slowly getting lower in the water. We managed to get everything aboard and evenly spread and slowly made our way back to Ramsgate. There was no room anywhere on the boat to do anything, so we just had to sit tight and wait. We couldn't even make a start at clearing the top of gear until we were back in port.

Once safely back in the harbour we tied up alongside a pontoon on the east pier so that we could run the gear off the boat. The three of us got stuck into the task ahead of us. It was now the middle of the night, it was freezing cold, and to top it all we had drunk alcohol which made it feel like it was even colder than it actually was.

We filled around a dozen boxes with herrings and I took them to the fish shop to at least give us a bit of space. Whilst I was there, I filled the van with empty boxes ready for the next lot. Once back at the boat I could see that we were not making a lot of progress. The lads were working hard but it was the sheer volume of fish that was slowing us up. I don't know how many trips I made with the van to get the fish to the market, but I do know that at the time we couldn't have cared less if we never saw another herring for as long as we lived.

We were putting more fish than we should have in each box, and by the time we had cleared everything out of the gear we had filled fifty seven boxes with a total of 347 stones of fish. We had also dumped about twenty stone of fish that had got crushed because they were at the bottom of the nets.

If these figures don't mean a lot to anyone, it was well over two ton of herrings that we had landed, and we had caught them whilst we were on the piss in the Tartar Frigate.

The news

Sticking with the herrings, I remember catching a load one year somewhere around 1990 and not being able to sell them. Fishing in general had been grim and we had turned to the herrings to try and make up for the shortage of other fish. We had been drifting for them at night and we were catching about twenty stone (around four boxes) of them with a value of about eighty to ninety quid. It was not a lot, but it was certainly better than nothing.

We set off from the harbour one night and set our gear to drift just off the coast. The conditions were perfect and my thoughts (which I kept to myself) were that we could easily end up catching eight or nine boxes. After our drift we started hauling the gear back. We had hit the jackpot, there were loads of herrings coming aboard. By the time we had got the last net in we had over 24 boxes of them.

Early the next morning I took them to Johnstone's fish shop in Broadstairs knowing that the price would be down from £4 a stone to £3 with the usual excuses about not being able to sell them all. I was miles out with my figure of three quid, I was offered a pound a stone for the lot! As you can imagine a heated row followed with me deciding to park up outside the shop and give them away rather than accepting his miserable offer.

You can't do that he screamed at me as I gave away the first dozen to which I replied, 'you just fucking watch me'. Anyway, as I was giving these fish away, I was slagging him off at the same time. He called a couple of traffic wardens over to make me move on. I soon sent them packing, I gave them a bag of herrings each and I promised them that I would be gone within the hour. About 45 minutes and a box of fish later I drove off knowing I was on a loser but satisfied that at least I had cost the fish shop a few customers.

I wasn't going to let it rest there, I phoned the local newspaper about it. They put a report entitled 'Best catch goes begging' complete with a photograph on the back page of the Thanet gazette. The next thing I knew, I received a phone call from Radio Kent. They wanted to do an interview on air for their audience to listen to which I immediately agreed to do. They met me later that day on the harbour wall and conducted the interview on the boat. I explained to them what had really pissed me off, and that was the fact that the price would crash for the fishermen, but the consumer never benefitted from the glut of fish because the price on the slab would stay the same. The radio station ended up having a phone in to find out who could find the dearest herring in the county.

A few days later we were having breakfast in a local café before we set off to sea. Three blokes came in, very official looking and suited and booted. One of them came over to our table and asked us, 'Does anyone know Steve Barratt because we are looking for him'. I was pretty sure that they were the CID so I politely answered him with 'Who's looking for him?' I was going to tell them that he was at sea fishing and wasn't due back for hours. 'TVS news' came the reply. I heaved a sigh of relief and said, 'It's your lucky day mate, you have just found him'

They had read the newspaper article and they had heard the radio report and wanted the story for the 6 'o' clock regional news. It didn't take long before they asked us if we could take them out on the boat and catch some fish to dump for the cameras. I explained to them that we didn't catch many herrings during the daylight hours because the fish were deeper in the water, and that it would be better to take them at night. Unfortunately, they couldn't wait because they had the news slot to fill so I agreed to take them on the understanding that there probably wouldn't be a lot of fish.

We left the harbour and cast our nets and then I did a televised interview whilst the gear was fishing. It wasn't a bad interview, but somehow, we had to find some fish to dump to do the interview justice. John, one of the guys that worked with me came up with a cunning plan. He had worked out how to strap a fish box on the outside of the boat without it being seen. We would be able to dump some fish over the side for the cameras without losing them.

It worked perfectly, we caught about a box and a half of fish and managed to dump them over the side four times! The camera crew were brilliant, nobody could possibly know what we had done because they managed to conceal the box on the outside completely. I can even remember some of the fishermen saying how surprised they were at the amount of fish we had caught with it being the wrong time of day to be fishing.

A very hard job

I remember working one year on a fishing boat called the 'Fairwind'. We were fishing for whelks. She was a lovely boat that had been built with an aft wheelhouse. This made it easy to see everything that was going on when hauling the gear. We used to take it in turns to get the gear in, John would haul a string on the hauler with me in the wheelhouse keeping the boat in the right position and then we would swap over for the next string and so on until we had hauled everything.

We were working at the time just off the low water mark between Deal and Pegwell Bay and on the day in question it was really hot with no wind at all and plenty of sunshine. I had taken my top off, and I was working with just a pair of shorts on and wellington boots. We were about half way through the day, I had hauled the last string of pots aboard, so it was my turn to do a stint in the wheelhouse. I could see a catamaran approaching us from the North and I could just make out a voice coming over some sort of a loudspeaker.

A local travel firm had invested in a passenger boat for pleasure trips and Nigel who was a good friend of ours had taken the job of skippering it. His job was to give holidaymakers a boat trip wherever he thought was the best place to take them and ensure that safety was paramount whilst people were on board. Nigel had been at sea locally for virtually all his working life, he had his own fishing boat, he was a very respected member of the Ramsgate Lifeboat crew, so without any doubt he was the right man for the job.

As this boat which was named the 'Marinair' got closer to us I was trying to think of something funny to do. I don't know why but I just decided to strip off to just my wellington boots. I ended up standing in the wheelhouse naked from the boots up and I was literally crying with laughter. John was out on the deck working and knew that I had taken my top off but had no idea whatsoever that I had stripped off completely.

Nigel slowed the 'Marinair' down with all the holiday makers peering out of the windows at us and taking photographs. He came to a halt about fifty metres away. I could hear him talking to the passengers on the ships loudspeaker system, he was explaining to them how we hauled up the whelk pots in strings of about thirty, about how heavy they were and how we emptied, baited and re-shot them. He finished off by telling them how hard the local fishermen worked to enable people to eat fresh local whelks.

As he finished his last sentence I jumped out of the wheelhouse, it was like something out of a comedy sketch. I was stark bollock naked and I was waving my hands and shouting at them. It was hilarious, John turned around to see what was going on and collapsed in a heap on the deck. He was rolled up, he couldn't stop laughing. The hauler kept going and a whelk pot flew into the boat and nearly took his head off. He was laughing so much he couldn't get up off the deck to turn the hauler off and I could see that this prank was going to end up with us having a serious accident if we didn't stop the hauler from pulling the pots in. I had no choice, I had to run from the wheelhouse to the front of the boat where the controls were with fuck all on but my wellies and turn the hydraulics off.

I have no idea what was going through the minds of the people watching us and whether anyone was filming it or not. One thing I did found out for sure was that Nigel was pissed off with me. He was extremely pissed off, he couldn't see the funny side of it at all, all he could see was himself being made to look a prat because he had gone to the trouble of explaining to everyone how hard we worked only for them to see me jumping up and down with all my tackle out on display.

Where have you been?

I decided to take the boat out and shoot about a half of our gear on a wreck to see if there was any cod there to be caught. The rest of the gear was to be shot on the open ground so that we would still earn a wage if the fish were not on the wreck. With this plan in mind we steamed for about an hour in an easterly direction and offloaded some gear to fish for skate and smooth hounds. We then continued heading east to try our luck and give the wrecks a go.

After about another hour I arrived at the wreck where I wanted to shoot the gear only to find a French fisherman had already put his nets on it. He was friendly enough, he tried to explain to me exactly how he had shot his gear so that I could get my gear on the wreck as well. It proved to be a none starter, his nets had been shot from east to west and I wanted to put mine from north to south. If I shot my gear it would have ended up on the top of him. I thanked him for trying to help and explained to him that it would be easier for me to go and shoot my gear on a different wreck.

I headed off to the south east and shot my gear on a couple of smaller wrecks that were about two miles away. As soon as I had finished shooting my gear I headed back to the Frenchman. The sea was like a sheet of glass and it would be no problem whatsoever to go alongside him with our boat. I got John to put us right next to the Frenchman and I climbed aboard him for a chat. We shook hands and he invited me into the wheelhouse where he promptly took a bottle of 'Pastis' and two glasses out of the cupboard.

Within a few minutes we were laughing and joking with a mixture of English and French words being strung together in some sort of sentences. The drink was going down a treat, it was the first time I had drunk Pastis (some sort of an aniseed drink which he had mixed with water) and in all fairness it tasted quite good. I stayed aboard him for a good couple of hours before shaking hands again and leaving to go and collect my gear.

We hauled the gear in and the amount of fish we caught certainly wasn't a record breaker. We did however end up with about a half dozen boxes of cod. This was a good enough sign to us to plan another trip out to the wrecks in the hope of being able to shoot on the wreck we had originally intended to fish. With that thought in mind we headed back towards the land and our gear that had been shot on the open ground.

We hauled back the remainder of our gear and as anticipated had a couple of boxes of skate and four or five boxes of smooth hounds to add to the cod and make the day up. Finally, with everything on board and the daylight disappearing quickly we headed back to port. By the time we were back at the harbour it was total darkness.

I made my way over to the steps on the east pier to unload our catch and as soon as we had got there and secured the boat all these people appeared out of the darkness. There were about a dozen of them, some in overalls, some in jeans and a couple that were suited and booted. One of the guys in a suit jumped on aboard us brandishing an identity badge and introduced himself as 'Her Majesty's Customs and Excise'.

To say I was pissed off was an understatement, we had had a very long day, we hadn't done anything wrong, we were tired, and we wanted to go home. Here we were in the middle of the night with a load of idiots on board our boat. The guy that had introduced himself to me asked me where we had been. I pointed to the harbour entrance and sarcastically said 'out there'. He then asked me what we had been doing to which I replied 'fishing'. I really wasn't in the mood for this, he then advised me that they would be doing a thorough search of my boat. I shrugged my shoulders and told him to crack on with it, I had nothing to hide.

I stepped off the boat and had a cigarette with the crew whilst they searched the boat. They seemed very frustrated because they couldn't find whatever it was that they were looking for. Only then did the penny drop and we realized what was going on. Dover coastguard must have seen two blips on their radar screen coming together in mid channel when I tied up alongside the Frenchman. I had later returned to the UK and he had returned to France. They must have thought that it was something suspicious and we were in the middle of a drugs shipment or something of the sort.

They kept searching and still they couldn't find anything. One of the customs guys put a pair of ultra-thin latex gloves on and my mate turned to me and said 'he ain't sticking his fingers up my arse'. As it happens that was not his intention, he had decided that we must have hidden whatever they were looking for in the fish boxes with the fish. He pushed his hand into a box of cod and had a good feel around to reveal nothing but fish. He then went through the rest of the cod. Following the cod, he searched through the boxes of dogfish still without any success.

The last fish box to be searched was the box with the skate in. They had been boxed white side up and there was no way on this earth I was going to tell him to be careful because the other side was covered in spikes. He pushed his hand in and had a good feel around and then tried to remove his hand. After a while he finally managed to get it out, the glove had been shredded by the spikes and he had blood pissing everywhere from the scratches on his hand. I looked at the guy in the suit smiled and said 'do you mind if we go home now'

Air guitar

I had a mate who was a fellow fisherman called Dave Turner, who sadly lost his life several years ago. He was a diabetic, I am not sure what his actual diagnosis was but often someone would find him either slumped in his chair or on the deck of his boat. We soon learned that it was nothing to be alarmed about, we would just wake him up and get him to eat a mars bar or something similar with a high sugar level. Once he had eaten, he would inject himself with some medicine with a syringe and within minutes he was back to normal.

I remember fishing for bass on one of the offshore sand banks in the Thames Estuary. There was quite a bit of fish there to be caught and unfortunately, at the time I only had one fleet of gear that was suitable to use to catch them. I discussed the situation with Dave and it turned out that he hadn't been catching much fish and had a fleet of gear the same as mine that he wasn't using. There was no point in us both taking our boats out to the sand bank with only one lot of gear each so he put his gear on my boat and we worked together for a while taking it in turns to skipper the boat.

It was a Friday and whilst we were on the way out to the sand bank we were chatting about what we were going to do over the weekend. I told him that I was going to a pub with karaoke that evening in a place called St. Nicholas. Dave had never been to a karaoke before, so I invited him along. It would be no problem for him to get there because it was about half way between the Harbour and where he lived in Herne Bay.

We finished work that day, weighed the fish in at the market and went home to get cleaned up and ready for the evening. I arranged to meet him at about half past eight and sure enough, when I got there shortly after eight his van was already in the car park. I met him inside and introduced him to my missus, Bob who ran the karaoke and various other people that I knew in there.

We had a few beers and laughed and joked about different things. The karaoke started just before nine and someone got up to sing. I put my name down on the list for a song and asked Dave if he was going to have a go. He wasn't very enthusiastic but said he might have a go later when he had had a few beers. There were several people there that night that were singing different types of songs and by about ten o clock Dave decided he was ready to have a go.

There was already a singer in the bar with the same name, so I got a request slip and wrote 'Dave the fish' at the top. That's you I said to him 'now what are you going to do'? I couldn't believe it when he replied with 'Smoke on the Water by Deep Purple' It was a brilliant song, but not the type of song you would expect someone to do that had never sung before. Bob slowly worked his way through the list of singers and then he made an announcement over the microphone, 'We have a new singer in the house tonight, please put your hands together for Dave the fish'

Dave said something like 'give me one minute' and ran out of the bar and into the car park. I thought he had bottled it but within seconds he was back with a bright red air guitar in his hand. He grabbed hold of me and he said something like 'Come on, you are doing the singing and I am playing the guitar!' This was a first, we hadn't had anyone on stage with an air guitar before. The music started, it is a song with a long guitar intro. Dave went mental, everyone in the pub was laughing and cheering at his performance, he really thought he was a rock star. At the end of the song he got the loudest applause of the whole evening and it became a weekly ritual for him to perform for everyone.

By the end of the evening he had drunk far too much alcohol to drive his van home, so we did a detour via Herne Bay and dropped him off on route. I arranged to pick him up at seven thirty in the morning to retrieve his van and catch the tide back out to the fishing grounds. When I called at his house the following morning he was still in the porch, exactly where I had left him, and he was still holding his big red blow up guitar!

The Fisherman

A poem I wrote back in the eighties when I was at sea in the 'Lady Sarah'

Its four in the morning the alarm clock rings
Out in the garden the dawn bird sings
Far of in the distance I hear the sound
Of the all-weather milkman doing his round

I drag myself out of my warm cosy bed
My eyes feeling sore and my legs feel like lead
Deep down I pray for wind and rain
So that I can go back to bed again

But the forecast is good just a nice gentle breeze
So I rush down some breakfast and pick up my keys
I open the door and glance at the clock
And then head for the boat which is down at the dock

At 5.30 sharp I leave on the tide
And for the next two hours a laborious ride
Between seven and eight I cast off my nets
And hope to catch fish to pay off some debts

By midday it's clear that the fishing is poor

So I'll try somewhere else and hope to catch more

At nine in the evening I finally get home

And jump in the bath and then search for a comb

I relax for an hour and talk to my wife

Then I'll go off to bed that's my way of life

I close my eyes and dream of sweet things

Then at four in the morning the alarm clock rings

It pays to answer the radio when called

I was fishing in the Thames Estuary on some of the wrecks that were in the Queens Channel for lobster in the late eighties. I had shot the nets on a Friday morning and the plan was to haul clear and re-shoot them on the Sunday over the slack tide.

We put to sea on the Sunday as planned and made our way to our fishing gear in the Estuary. As we got closer to our destination I was horrified to see a very large beam trawler working in the vicinity of our gear. I tried to call the boat on several different VHF channels but could not raise a response. I even called them on Channel sixteen as I felt sure that they would be monitoring this channel whilst trawling in a busy shipping lane. It didn't seem to make any difference what I did, I was blatantly being ignored.

I had no choice other than to contact the local fisheries department about the incident which I promptly did on the boats 'mobile' phone. I have put mobile in inverted comma's because it was mobile in name only, it was more like a fixture on the boat with a battery nearly as big as what would be needed to start a car engine.

The fact that this fishing vessel was breaking the law and was fishing inside the three mile limit did not bother me at all because we all bend the rules at times to try and earn a living. What bothered me was the situation I was in whereby this vessel could have literally towed my gear away and because of the size of it would not even had known he had done it. All I needed was the bloke to answer me and reassure me that my gear was ok where I had shot it and he could have fished there unhindered for as long as he wanted to.

What resulted from my telephone call to the local fisheries department was a court case against the vessel for illegal fishing activities. The case went to court several months later at Margate Magistrates Court with myself my crew John and Stuart who was just a school lad at the time being summonsed to court to give evidence.

We met up beforehand at a café just around the corner from the courthouse. Whilst ordering our teas and coffees I spotted four or five guys sat around a table with a full size chart of the Thames Estuary spread out in front of them. I went and sat at the table next to them, it was obviously the people we were up in court against. Very quickly I established from their conversation that their main line of defence was the fact that their equipment was a lot more expensive than mine and therefore more accurate and I had reported them as being inside the three mile limit when in fact they weren't.

We entered the court and my advice to John and Stuart was to just tell the truth and not try and fabricate anything. The case proceeded and one by one we were called up to give evidence. When I was called their barrister tried to put me in a corner. As I expected, he asked me about the equipment on my boat and the value of it. He then asked me if I had checked the reading it was giving me whilst we were in the harbour to make sure it was working properly. I confirmed that I had not in fact done this and he summed up his questioning of me by saying 'I put it to you that on the day in question your equipment was faulty and was transmitting the wrong position to you'. I turned to the judge and said 'If what this guy is saying is correct, the wrecks that I was fishing have managed to move half a mile because the gear was on exactly the same numbers as the ones I had written in my log book on the Friday and I had checked my equipment that day.

They were found guilty and fined £2000.00 with £300.00 costs. The funny thing was the fact that it was December when the case went to court and there was a north east gale blowing. We would not have been able to go to sea and the £300.00 costs that they had to pay was to give me £150.00 John £100.00 and young Stuart (who should have been at school) £50.00 for loss of earnings for the day.

Dan Air

I have been back to Jersey on loads of occasions. Sometimes I went by plane, sometimes I went by ferry and on one occasion I even took my own boat (I was fully prepared for the journey this time with proper charts and a planned route!). I have written about a few of them in this section whether I was visiting for work or pleasure or both.

I had often talked at home to Debi about my experiences and friends in Jersey and we decided to book a holiday there with the kids. Money was a bit tight, so we chose a budget airline flying to Jersey from Gatwick called 'Dan Air' and we booked to stay on a campsite not far from the airport once we got there. The site had everything we needed, a fully equipped and erected tent complete with all the usual kitchen stuff, a cooker and a fridge. In addition to this there was a swimming pool, a children's club, a small shop and a bar on site.

The kids were very young, in fact Lauren was still a baby, and the plan was to spend most of the time on and around the campsite and hire a car for a few days (I knew that the hire charges were low on the island) to do the usual sightseeing and visit friends.

To cut a long story short, we had a fabulous holiday with excellent weather and some good quality family time together. Unfortunately, it was that good that before we knew it, the holiday was over and we were packing up our stuff and making our way to the airport for our flight back to the UK.

We checked our bags in without any problems, confirmed with the airport staff that our flight was on time and went to the relevant gate to await boarding instructions. Everything went to plan, and the plane was loaded and ready to take off exactly as per its schedule.

We all buckled up and listened to the safety instructions and then the plane left Jersey for the short flight to Gatwick. Some 45 minutes later I began to wonder if something was wrong, by now we should have been on the ground and we hadn't even started to make our descent. In deed there was something wrong, Gatwick was hidden somewhere below a dense fog bank and the pilot had been instructed to circle the airport and await instructions as it was impossible to land safely.

An hour passed by and we were still going around in circles. By now Lauren had started to get irritable, it had passed her feeding time and we had nothing to give her! All her food was in our suitcases in the hold. Another hour passed and still we circled the airport along with a lot more aircraft that we could see out of the windows doing the same. We circled the airport for four hours awaiting instructions to land. Lauren was in a right state by now and was permanently screaming or crying for food. This short flight had turned into a complete nightmare.

Everybody on board was getting pissed off by now, when there was a crackle, and a message came through the speaker system on board from the Captain. We were now running dangerously low on fuel and we were going to be diverted to another airport so that we could land. The airport was either going to be Bournemouth or Manston and he would keep us informed. I was hoping for Manston, it was only a couple of miles from where we lived. Debi could take the kids home and I would somehow get back to Gatwick to collect our car.

Luck was not on our side and we ended up at Bournemouth. We were given light refreshments in the terminal and told to wait for further instructions. Fortunately, we managed to find some food for Lauren and calm her down. Rowanne had been no trouble at all, it had all seemed like a bit of an adventure to her.

A tiring day was just about to get a lot worse, the Captain came over to everyone with some important developments. He said something like 'we have a problem folks, the plane has been impounded for an unpaid fuel bill in the past! We will have to collect our bags from the aircraft and await coaches to get us all back to Gatwick'. It was unbelievable, the plane had literally been confiscated by the airport.

What had started out as a journey that should have taken just over half an hour was now in its ninth hour!

Coaches did turn up eventually to ferry us all back to Gatwick and some eleven hours after the start of our journey we did finally make it back to our car only to find that it had a flat battery and wouldn't start!

Unpaid parking Fine

After being back in the UK for around six years I had the urge to return to Jersey again for another holiday. There was no problem with the boat, the lads were going to continue fishing with it whilst I was away. This technically meant that I was having a paid holiday for a change assuming that they caught some fish. Normally, I would leave the boat tied up when I was away, so it would be earning nothing.

I was travelling on this occasion on my own and by far the cheapest way for me to get to Jersey was to catch the overnight ferry from Portsmouth to St. Helier. I can't remember how I got to the ferry terminal, I think it might have been by coach, but this was the route I took. It was a very pleasant crossing and I was able to have a few beers on board as I didn't have to worry about driving at the other end.

The ferry docked in Jersey and I joined the queue to exit the terminal via the local customs booths. People were being cleared quickly until it was my turn. My passport was checked, some words were said amongst the customs officers there and then I was taken with my bag to one side. Once away from the public they started treating me like a criminal. I couldn't work out what was wrong and what I could possibly have done.

Finally, one of the officers read me my rights and advised me that I was going to be arrested for none payment of a parking fine. I was gob smacked, how could a stupid fine that was issued over six years ago still be registered on the system. I pleaded my innocence, but they were not really interested. In the end, I had to make a phone call to a friend that was a Jersey resident and they had to come down to the Customs Department at the ferry terminal and bail me out.

Once she had spoken to the officers and signed some paperwork, I was free to go and ordered to attend the local court the following Thursday morning to answer to the charge I was being accused of in front of a judge. I left the terminal with Amanda and she made it very plain to me that whatever the outcome I did have to attend the hearing. Failure to turn up would result in her getting in trouble with the law. I promised her I would be at the hearing and that was the end of our discussion on this matter.

I was having a great time on the island, catching up with old friends, plenty of drinking, and I even did a couple of days work on one of the fishing boats. Thursday came around, and as promised I attended the court house. I was on holiday, so I didn't have a suit, I just went as smartly dressed as possible. I signed in at the reception desk and was given instructions as to where the waiting room was. I was advised that my name would be called shortly, and I would be taken to stand in front of the judge to answer to the said charge.

Sure enough, within twenty minutes I found myself stood in front of a judge and the alleged offence was read out to me. That being the fact that a vehicle that was registered in my name that I had owned nearly seven years ago had been issued with a parking fine for not having a parking ticket on display, I had not made the relevant payment, and to date this payment was still outstanding.

I was then asked by the judge if I had anything to say about the matter. I told him that I had sold the vehicle around the time of the offence, and that there were not any outstanding fines on it. I went on to tell him that it looked like the fine had been issued after the vehicle had been sold and possible the new owner had not changed the details with the vehicle licensing centre. It was possible that he had ignored the fine knowing the vehicle was still registered in my name and that I had returned for good to live in the UK.

I then went on to tell him that I loved Jersey, and I would not have deliberately avoided paying a fine. I concluded by telling him that this whole matter had caused me a lot of stress and ruined my holiday.

The judge was silent for a minute and then he ended up apologising to me for the inconvenience I had been subjected to, and he offered me £25 in compensation so that I could enjoy the rest of my holiday!

Colin the crab

Following on from my previous visit, I went home armed with the knowledge that I could loan a small fishing boat (a Cygnus 21) from a guy who used to supply a lot of the local lads with their fishing gear. I had explained to him that I wanted to try a bit of net fishing on the island and he was only too pleased to let me use his boat. It was a perfect scenario, I could experiment with some nets, and if I was successful in any way, he would receive a percentage of the profit. In addition to this he would get the order for any nets I needed to buy in the future.

After several months back in Thanet, I decided to take him up on his offer. I telephoned him to confirm that the offer still stood and then set about sorting out what gear I was going to take with me. I loaded my car with small amounts of all different types of gear, the plan being to find out what sort worked best out there and then to maximize our catch by concentrating on that gear.

I had a mate Nigel Stephens who came with me, he was up for a change and had heard some of my stories from when I had previously lived there. After a few last minute arrangements, we were ready to head off to Jersey, we had a boat to work, we had a selection of gear in the boot of the car, and we had been told we could stay at Ricky and Caroline's whilst we were there.

We arrived safely and immediately went to the Folie for a few beers. I took this opportunity to introduce Nigel to the landlord and some of my friends. We then headed off to Ricky's to unload our clothes and toiletries. We had already decided on treating them to a take away for putting us up followed by an early night in anticipation of the following day being an eventful one.

Nice and early the next morning we were up and away. The first thing I did was to collect the keys from Bob (the boat owner) and then I took Nigel to check it out. It was fine, just what we needed to try out a bit of netting on the island. There were already a few nets on the boat, so with these and the ones we had brought with us we set to sea to do some fishing. We shot three of four lots of gear, returned to the harbour and then retired to the pub with the plan being to collect them the following day.

Having had a good night's sleep, we awoke to glorious sunshine and eagerly got ourselves ready to go and haul the gear. We caught a few fish, it was nothing spectacular but the fish we did catch were absolute prime. We had dover soles that weighed more than 2kg each and plaice that went over 3kg. We could only imagine that these fish were so big because nobody had fished for them. It seemed at the time that all the boats earned a living on crab and lobster with pots.

We didn't catch any lobsters on our first day, but we did catch some huge spider crabs. They were that big that it was hard to imagine how they could get themselves caught in a pot, the backs on them were wider than the entrances to the pots. This got us thinking, could we earn a living by fishing for crab that was too big to get caught in a pot? It was an exciting thought and played a big part in the way we fished from there on.

After a week of experimenting with the gear in different places we decided that loads of big mesh gear and concentrating on spider crabs would be the way forward. I borrowed a van from a friend, and we returned to England with it to fill it up with skate nets I had in storage at Ramsgate. Nigel was so impressed with the size of the crabs we were catching he packed a live one in ice to take back with us.

We caught the ferry to the mainland to spend a few days at home and load up the van. On arrival at Portsmouth we were immediately directed to the Customs pound. Once there I was told that I could not take the van any further. They gave me some bullshit about import duty and VAT having not been paid. I tried to explain to them that I was returning to Jersey in less than a week, I even showed them my ferry ticket to verify that I was telling the truth.

They were having none of it, I offered to pay the VAT. This only seemed to make matters worse with him sarcastically asking me where I would find that kind of money. I took it out of my pocket and showed him a wedge of cash and went on to tell him that I was a fisherman and claimed all my VAT payments back. He didn't like the fact that he could do all this work for Customs and Excise only for me to reclaim it all back. We had hit a brick wall and we had no choice other than to leave the van there until we returned to Jersey and catch a train for the rest of our journey home.

We headed for the station with our bags and a large icebox containing Nigel's crab. Once on board we settled down with a few cans of beer for the journey home which was via Waterloo in London. Part way through the trip I went off to the toilet and on my return, I couldn't believe my eyes. Some people had moved out of the carriage to sit elsewhere and a couple that were sat adjacent to us had put their feet up on the table.

Nigel was in hysterics, and in between fits of giggles he said' 'I hope you don't mind but I have let Colin out for a while so that he can stretch his legs!' We were only on the train to Waterloo station with a 4kg spider crab on the loose!

Six weeks in the nick.

We had mixed results with the boat that we had loaned, and we used it on and off for good couple of months. A few years later I returned to Jersey with my own boat the 'Lady Sarah' and a mountain of fishing gear. This time it was going to be make or break, fishing had been very poor at Ramsgate and I had ended up several months behind with my boat loan repayments. In addition to that, we had decided to get married and the wedding was getting closer, so I had that to pay for as well and it was proving to be rather expensive.

I took Guildy with me, and I can always remember the way I felt as we steamed out of Ramsgate harbour. Rowanne and Lauren were stood at the end of the pier waving frantically at us, and we had no idea how long it would be that we were away. I waved back and blew them a kiss and then headed straight towards Dover without looking back, if I had I would have turned the boat around and not gone. On arrival at St. Helier some 35 hours later we tied up in the Collette yacht basin for the night and made our way straight to the Folie to let everyone know that we were there and of course for a few beers.

Within an hour of getting there, a friend had loaned us a van for the duration of our stay. Someone else's boat had been craned out for a month and we were told that we could use his mooring so that we would not be charged as he had fully paid up for the year. As if things could not have got any better, we were given somewhere to stay for the next six weeks. One of the fisherman's brother was a prison officer at the islands one and only prison. He was married to an Irish lady and she had gone back to Ireland with the kids to visit her family over the school holidays meaning his house was empty

We soon got ourselves into a daily routine, breakfast first thing in the morning in the pier café, then out in the boat for most of the day fishing, and then off to the fish market with our catch before having a few beers in the Folie and driving home.

I don't know how we got away with it, we were driving a van that quite possibly was illegal, we didn't even know if we had insurance and we were taking it in turns to drive it home after drinking several pints of beer. Talk about taking the piss, we used to drive up to the gates at the entrance to the prison, and wave to the guards that were on duty. They would wave back at us and about thirty seconds later these massive gates would swing open for us. Once inside the compound the gates would close behind us and then we had to drive past all the prison cells and on to the prison officer's quarters which was where we were staying.

Probably the best organised BBQ's ever

The fishermen in Jersey were very family orientated and it was very rare for them to work on a Sunday, they preferred to take the day off and spend it with their wives and kids.

We were drinking in the Folie one Sunday morning and arrangements were being finalized for a BBQ that was taking place the following week. I was invited along with Guildy and we accepted the invitation. It seemed a bit expensive at the time, it was about fifteen quid. We shrugged our shoulders, paid the money and we were told that we had to be ready to board a coach at 10.30 sharp the following Sunday.

Everything went to plan, and a full coach comprising mainly of families set off from the pub to take us to a venue on the north side of the island. The coach driver drove down some small and windy country lanes and then pulled over to let us off in a clearing surrounded by trees.

Once we had disembarked from the coach we had a look around and were pleasantly surprised with what we saw. There was an endless line of bongo's (45 gallon plastic drums) that contained ice and had been filled with bottles and cans of beer. A volleyball court had been constructed for the kids to play on, several BBQ's were lit and ready to start cooking and to top it all a DJ was setting his gear up in the back of a Luton van to provide us with entertainment.

All of a sudden, £15 did not seem like such a bad deal. It looked like there was as much food as we could possibly eat, beer, entertainment and transport thrown in. It was a fabulous day, we played several games of volley ball with the youngsters, between drinking copious amounts of beer, we had good music which went on till very late in the evening and everyone kids included was in high spirits.

Around about midnight everyone started mucking in to clean the place up of any mess that we might have made. We joined in and before long the place was spotless. An 'AA' van turned up with its amber lights flashing and pulled up next to the DJ's Luton. I assumed that he was having difficulty getting his van started. When I made enquiries as to what the problem was, I found out that in actual fact there was nothing wrong with his van. The DJ was pissed like the rest of us and the AA were here to tow it back to St. Helier with all his equipment on board.

I suggested a whip round to give the guy a drink for turning out only to be told that it had all been arranged a week earlier and that part of our £15 was to pay for it!

On another occasion, a BBQ was being organised to take place on a secluded beach a few miles west of the harbour. There was no access from anywhere on the land to the beach, the only way to get to it was via boat. The plan was to ferry everyone across the bay in a couple of the bigger fishing boats and then to take everyone ashore by dinghy. After the success of the last BBQ we booked ourselves straight in for it. We did feel a bit like we were not really family, so we took the 'Lady Sarah' over to where it was all happening rather than jumping aboard one of the other two boats with everyone else.

Once off the beach, they anchored up and they started carefully ferrying the kids ashore in the dinghies. The beach didn't appear to be rocky, it was mainly sand, and I decided that it was just as easy to ram the boat up the beach as it was to anchor it off. It was easy to do as the boat had been built with bilge keels so that it could be moored in a tidal harbour. The two bigger boats were not able to do this, had they tried it they would have rolled over on to one side when the water dropped away.

I went alongside one of the boats, told them what I was going to do, and they passed all the food, drink, plates, cutlery and equipment over. I also helped a couple of my mate's kids climb on board. Once everything was loaded up, I steamed the boat straight onto the beach and as soon as the tide ebbed away we unloaded everything. The boat just sat there for the day until the tide came in again. A new name was born there and then. My boat was registered in Ramsgate, and I had literally rammed it up the beach. Any BBQ's planned to be held on the beach in the future were always organised with the bulk of the stuff being transported there aboard the 'Ramsgate Ram'.

You look worse than she did!

We had been in Jersey for about four weeks and Jimmy had travelled out to join us. Life was pretty good, we worked hard, we drank hard and we played hard as well. We were miles away from home, so we didn't have to answer to anyone. I remember being in the pub one night and I was chatting to a local girl that I had got quite friendly with over the previous couple of weeks. The two of us left the pub to go for a stroll together along the coast leaving Guildy and Jimmy behind.

We ended up perched quite high on some rocks overlooking the harbour flirting with each other when we couldn't believe our eyes. Jimmy had left the pub shortly after us and he had walked down onto the beach amongst the boats that were moored there. It was hilarious, he had no idea that he was being watched, and he had stripped off to go skinny dipping. We were laughing together watching him and wondering how and where he thought he was going to go swimming, it was a spring tide and the bloody sea was miles away.

He staggered off in the right general direction of the water, he was totally naked and singing away to himself at the top of his voice. He eventually found the sea, and he walked in up to his waist and had a good splash around. After about five minutes he came out of the sea and started walking back up the beach. He soon found out he had a problem, he wasn't walking in the direction of his clothes! We watched him for a good half hour before he finally located the spot where he had left them and managed to get himself dressed.

Later that evening, not knowing whether the boys had gone back to the prison or not we made our way to the boat which was tied up in the marina and she stayed the night. Without going into detail, it turned into a fully blown session before we both dosed off. I woke at about five in the morning and the first thing that entered my head was 'oh fuck, what have we gone and done, this wasn't supposed to happen'.

I had someone at home that I was due to get married to, and a couple of lovely kids. She had several relatives including her dad that lived and worked either for the harbour or for the neighbouring businesses. As good as what had happened was, it needed to be kept quiet. We certainly couldn't afford to have everyone knowing about it.

We decided that the best thing we could do was to leave the boat separately. She would leave the boat by 5.30am before all the fishermen turned up and about twenty minutes later, I would follow her, and we would just happen to bump into each other at the Pier café. This she did, I watched her walk along the pontoon and out of the marina, and then up on to the harbour wall. I continued to watch her until she disappeared behind some buildings. I hung on for another five or ten minutes, I smoked a fag and then I left the boat as well. I walked the pontoon, I briefly said 'hello' to a couple of blokes that were on the way down to their boat, and up onto the harbour wall. Just like she did, I set off in the direction of the café as planned.

As I made my way past the pilot boat office three of the pilots ran out of their office and onto a balcony that was their lookout. I knew one of them quite well, a guy called Archie and he shouted out to me 'Fuck me Steve you look worse than she did!' I gave him a smile and carried on walking towards the cafe thinking to myself 'it's not even six in the morning and the bloody cat is out of the bag'

Over the course of the next five or six weeks we became very close and spent a lot of time together. This had turned into a relationship and I ended up with my head in a complete and utter mess. I couldn't work out what to do, I was beating myself up for days, even weeks. I had a nice house back in Thanet, I could picture the kids waving me off at Ramsgate, I thought about the bedtime stories I used to read to them at night, and I decided that although life was being good to me in Jersey and I was enjoying myself I had to knock it on the head and return home. We left the island pretty abruptly, and who knows, had my circumstances been different from what they were I would probably have stayed, and I could possibly have still been there today!

Nile bike ride

It was 1997 and I decided to do a charity bike ride along the Nile in Egypt. I had never been to North Africa and it seemed like a good idea to visit the pyramids and start seeing parts of the world other than places in Europe.

I got an enrolment pack from 'Mencap' and set about training in the gym and raising the required sponsorship money to qualify for the ride. It was great, I had never done anything like this before and it was something to look forward to. I had booked the ride about six months in advance but in what seemed like a very short space of time the date was upon me to take on this challenge.

I can't remember if it was Gatwick or Heathrow airport where we were to meet up, but the instructions were simple, I was to wear one of the tee shirts supplied for the event and just go and find and introduce myself to anyone else with the same tee shirt on. As per the norm, I found a few guys in the bar and before long we were all chatting about the upcoming week. I got on especially well with a bloke named Roy Valentine. We got on so well that other people joining us just assumed we were life-long friends and had planned the trip together.

We all checked in, grabbed a few bottles of blue Smirnoff from the duty free and before we knew it we were airborne and on our way to Egypt. It got quite messy on the plane, we had plenty of strong vodka and nothing to mix it with so by the time we arrived in Egypt we could hardly stand. We landed at Luxor airport where a coach was waiting to take us to a Nile cruiser which was to be our base for the next eight days. We were staying on board and the boat was to follow us as we cycled through the day and be ready for us at each point we stopped at.

Finally, after drinking at the airport in the UK, drinking on the plane, drinking on the coach during our transfer, we arrived at our boat the 'Princess Diana' where the crew were eagerly waiting to greet us and show us to the bar for free drinks!

We drank until about four in the morning and then headed for our cabins as we had a 10 'o' clock start the next day. I jumped in my bed, fell asleep and before I knew it the ships siren sounded off and it was time to get up and go and eat breakfast. I headed for the restaurant where I found everyone laughing and joking and appearing to ignore me. It was strange, I couldn't work out what was wrong, it certainly felt like something was. Anyway, I grabbed a plate and queued up to get some food. When I got to the counter and looked at what food was on offer I became even more confused. There was soup, prawns, steaks, vegetables in fact there was just about anything you could think of apart from bacon egg and toast.

I put some stuff on my plate, grabbed some cutlery and sat down at a table where several other people were eating. I tucked into my food and listened in on their conversation, I couldn't believe what I was hearing. They had all had breakfast, collected and adjusted their bikes and done the first twenty miles of the bike ride. I had slept through it all, it wasn't breakfast I was eating, it was my fucking evening meal. My saving grace was Roy, he appeared in the restaurant about twenty minutes behind me looking bleary eyed and had done exactly the same as I had and slept through the first day.

After eating, we found the guys in charge, explained the situation to them and were taken to the bike store to get kitted out for the rest of the week.

The next few days were fine, very tiring and very hot but also very enjoyable. We were cycling about sixty to seventy miles each day. The temperature was in the low forties and I have never sweated so much in my life. I calculated that I was drinking at least nine litres of water a day just while cycling.

One night after a long day there was several of us in the bar on board and the conversation got around to fund raising and how people had gone about it. Some people had held events such as quizzes, some had got their firms to sponsor them, one guy had even paid the sponsorship money himself as he didn't want the aggravation of fund raising. In total there was 110 of us on the ride and one of the riders was Carol Thatcher, Maggie Thatcher's daughter. I had had quite a few drinks, I nudged Roy so as to let him know I was on a wind up and told them that I was being sponsored by the Daily Mirror. They had agreed to pay me two thousand quid to obtain some photo's of Thatcher's Snatch.

For the next two days of the ride I jumped off my bike with a disposable camera and followed her every time she headed for the bushes to relieve herself. It was hilarious, loads of them really did think I was seriously trying to take some photographs of her, and I suspect that to this day they still do.

In a nutshell, I had a fabulous time, it was a great experience and it prompted me to do other bike rides in such places as India, Holland, Belgium and France some of which I am going to write about in this last bit of the book.

India bike ride

About two years after the bike ride in Egypt I decided to do another one, so I enrolled again, this time the ride was in India and was going to take ten days. The fundraising target was quite a bit higher for this event. This did not worry me, I had already decided how I was going to raise the money to qualify. I had raised most of the funds for the Egypt ride by designing a plaque which I has sold to various local businesses. It consisted of a framed photo taken on the ride and an it was engraved with something like 'A huge thankyou to (name of company) for your generous support for this event.' I would simply design another plaque for India instead of Egypt.

I contacted several people who I had made friends with on the Nile ride to see who was up for another one. A few of them thought it was a great idea and enrolled, unfortunately Roy couldn't make it but did offer to buy one of my plaques with his company name on it.

We all had about six months to prepare ourselves and raise the money needed to go and then just like the last time, before we knew it the departure date was upon us. Roy lived near Heathrow airport which was handy, it meant I could travel up the day before we flew and have a few beers with him. It also meant that I had somewhere to leave the car whilst I was away without having to pay a fortune to park it.

The flight to India took a lot longer than Egypt and we had a stop off for a couple of hours in Jordan on route. It was strange, I had never been to an airport before where you couldn't buy a beer! I can't remember how long the journey took, but it was certainly tiring and to top that, we had a transfer of at least three hours to our hotel once we had cleared immigration control.

On arrival at the hotel we were booked in, shown our rooms and told to meet up in the lounge an hour later for a briefing about the ride and overnight stops etc. At this point I realised that it was going to be completely different to the ride in Egypt. We had to pack our stuff up every morning, vacate our rooms and load our stuff onto a lorry as opposed to going off for a ride and having our hotel room follow us along the river bank.

I found India very educational, I had never seen class distinction on such a scale before. People were either obscenely rich or had absolutely nothing to their name. There was no-one in between, people were living in huge mansions with other people living under tarpaulin sheets at the end of their driveways. To this day I cannot understand how this was an acceptable way for people to treat each other, it was nothing short of shocking.

Anyway, getting back to the bike ride, we were fortunate enough to be off the tourist track and we saw India as it really was and not as is seen in a holiday resort such as Goa. Our ride started at the base of the Himalaya's and ended up in the heart of Delhi.

One day, early on in the journey we were cycling in the mountains and our route had a nine mile section on it that was downhill all the way to a village where we stopped for lunch. We were then given the option of either cycling back up or putting our bikes on a lorry and travelling back up on coaches. Most people opted for the coaches, but twelve of us decided to cycle it. I must have been mad, I was older than the other lads I wasn't as fit and one of only a few that smoked.

We set off an hour before the coaches with the aim of making it to Shimla on our bikes. The task in front of us was daunting, we had to climb nearly 1600 metres over the next nine miles. It was painful, it never seemed to level out and about two thirds of the way up I was totally wiped out. I told the guy cycling alongside me to go on as I couldn't make it. He refused to leave me and literally talked me through the pain. To make things worse, the coaches came past us cheering and waving as they went. I don't think I have ever experienced so much voluntary pain in my life.

Eventually, I realized that I was going to make it and found some strength from somewhere to keep peddling. We made it to Shimla and headed straight for the bar to celebrate. There was one guy on the ride that reckoned he was a tri-athlete and super fit. He was getting on everyone's nerves, we were all here for the crack and he thought he was superior to us. He came up to me in the bar and in a loud and sarcastic voice said, 'What did it feel like when we came past you on the coaches?'. I took a mouthful of drink, looked around and saw that everyone was listening and replied in an equally loud voice 'Better than being on the coach'. It was great, everyone roared with laughter and he shut up for the rest of the week.

Towards the end of our trip we stopped at a place near Delhi and went out for a meal. The food was outstanding, the atmosphere was great, and the beer was plentiful. Everyone was in high spirits, barring an absolute catastrophe we were all going to complete our epic journey. I excused myself and went to find the toilet. Eventually I found it and entered. To this day I have never seen anything like it, the toilet was overflowing with shit. It didn't have one, but the shit was as high as where the toilet seat would have been, and the stench was stomach churning. To top it all, someone was washing the dishes that we had eaten off in the sink right next to it. It was disgusting and all I could think was what dirty bastards they must have been to live and work like this.

I had a quick pee and returned to the group I was with. I told them what I had seen and a few of them went to check for themselves as they didn't believe me. Before we left to return to our hotel I nipped back to the toilet and took a photo of the disgusting state it was in.

We completed our trip and returned home. After about a week of being home I got my photo's back from the developers and set about sorting the plaques out. Fifteen plaques had the same photo put in them, that being a photo of me in the Himalaya's stood by my bike with a bunch of Indian kids next to me. The message on the plaque read something like 'Mencap would like to thank you for your kind generosity.

I just couldn't resist the temptation, and out of my own money I had a second plaque made up for Roy. It simply said, 'You didn't miss much mate' and had the photo of the toilet full of shit on it. I spoke to him several weeks later and he informed me that he had put it up in the pub and everyone was still laughing about it.

Riding with the old Bill

I made friends with a local copper called Ken that was on the India bike ride, had I gone on the Egypt ride a fortnight before I did, we would have met then. A group of the guys that he worked with used to go out for a bike ride around different parts of the county pretty well every month. About three times a year a bunch of around twenty of them, some of them with their husbands or wives used to go for long weekends cycling somewhere in Europe.

Ken managed to wangle it for me to be able to go with them and I did on numerous occasions cycling around the Kent countryside. I also joined them whenever I could on their rides on the other side of the channel. The outings were always very well planned out and we cycled to Le Touquet and Bologne in France, Ostende, Du Panne and Bruge in Belgium, and Sluisse in Holland to name but a few.

I remember one outing that involved a good 45 to 50 mile ride from the ferry terminal in Calais to Du Panne in Belgium. It was a very difficult ride due to adverse weather conditions and a force seven head on North East wind blowing. Several people were clearly struggling to cope with the weather and not enjoying the ride at all. One by one they dropped out and opted to get in the support vehicle that accompanied us.

It did cross my mind to join them but thought it only fair to not take up a seat that somebody else might need more than me. I joined up with three guys that had decided to push on to the hotel and we left the stragglers behind.

On arrival at our hotel we checked in and showered before heading to the bar for a few beers whilst we waited for the rest of the party to turn up. One thing I can confirm about the whole bunch of coppers that I was with is to say that they all liked to have a good drink and I mean a good drink. I am not sure why, but I assume that they find it easier to relax when they are away rather than being in a bar in their home town with the possibility of some arsehole walking in that they had nicked the week before.

Like I said earlier, some of them had their spouses with them and some were glad to get away on their own. One of the coppers had his daughter with him who I believe was training to be a solicitor. I found out later in the evening that it was her birthday and after a good night with everyone with excellent food and plenty of alcohol ended up back at her room with a bottle of Southern Comfort to celebrate her birthday.

I thought it best to go back to my room before everyone started to get up in the morning so at about six o clock I quietly opened the door and walked out into the corridor. No prizes for guessing who came out into the corridor at the same time as I did, yes it was, her fucking dad and to make matters worse, as I walked off towards my room she shouted out from behind the door, 'Thanks for a great night Steve!'

She was a lovely looking girl and very well proportioned. I spent the next two days with half of the group looking envious and wanting to know what had gone on in the bedroom and the other half giving me daggers. To sum things up in a nutshell, a very respected copper had taken his daughter to Europe for a nice trouble free cycling holiday and she had taken someone that he didn't know anything about back to her room for the night.

On another outing we cycled along the coast from Calais to Bologne where we were going to spend the night. As was the norm, we booked into our hotel and showered after spending the day in the saddle. We ate in the restaurant there before hitting the town for a few beers. After visiting several of the local bars we eventually found one that had loud music and dancing that looked like it would be open late.

We all piled in and after several more beers ended up on the dancefloor with some of the local girls. One of the higher ranking officers danced several times with one of them. The music slowed down, and he became quite intimate with her, in fact his hands were all over her. After several smooches she returned to her group of friends and he came back to sit with us with a great big grin on his face. I couldn't help it, I had spotted something that wasn't quite right. I turned to him and said something to the effect of 'I bet I can wipe that smile off your face' to which he laughed and replied 'Why is that, jealousy will get you nowhere'

With several of the others looking on and waiting for the punchline I said to him 'That sexy bird with the big tits you have been all over has got an Adam's apple'. The look on his face when he realized I was being serious was priceless. He made the others promise to never ever mention it when they got back to the nick, stating that 'What goes on tour stays on tour.

London to Brighton

The London to Brighton annual bike ride was one that I had fancied doing for several years, but it was one that I couldn't really organize due to the logistics of the ride and where I actually lived.

To start with, I had to get myself and my bike to South East London for the start of the ride, and then, assuming I made it to the finish line (it was only fifty odd miles so I couldn't see any real problem there) I would be faced with the task of somehow getting myself and my bike back home from Brighton to Margate.

Out of the blue one day I had a telephone call from my brother Jon. He was arranging to do the London to Brighton ride with some of his mates and wondered if I would be interested in joining them. At the time he was living about half way along the route approximately eight miles south of Crawley.

They made a really good job of organizing the day with transport provided at both ends. The idea was to meet up early at my brother's house, bundle everyone and their bikes into the back of a Luton van and get dropped off a couple of miles from the registration point. Once we were all out of the van the guy driving it was going to take it to Brighton and spend the day there and then meet us at the finish line to get us all safely back to my brother's place.

I didn't hesitate, I jumped at the opportunity, it was probably going to be the only realistic chance I would ever have of doing the ride. I registered the next day and set about raising a few quid for the charity that was recognised for hosting the event, that being the 'British Heart Foundation'

The night before the ride I drove from home to my brothers and stayed there to be fresh for the morning. We had a few beers and then we got an early night. The following morning, we loaded up the van between mugs of tea and bacon rolls and once done set off for London. Most of us had piled in the back of the van and we couldn't see a thing, we had no idea whatsoever of where we were or how busy it was until the driver decided to pull over and let us out.

When he did so he rolled the shutter up and we all jumped out. It was an amazing sight, I had never seen so many cyclists before in my life, there were thousands of them. The atmosphere was electric.

Wherever you looked there were smiling cyclists, most of them with their registration number pinned onto their shirts. If the numbers I could see were anything to go by there was more than twenty thousand people taking part in this event!

The organizers did an absolutely superb job, they had time allocations for different groups of numbers and were setting people off at around 10 minute intervals. I can't remember what our allocated time was to leave, I think it was around the middle of the morning, but I do remember that we had a plan we were going to keep to once we were underway.

It was quite a simple plan, we were going to clear the main London roads and then about five miles into the country we were stopping for a few beers at a nice village pub. We got there in two's and three's and basically regrouped. The couple of beers planned turned into five or six and I remember some silly girl lecturing us about drinking and cycling being dangerous. This is just what you need when you are out having a bit of fun, someone who reckons they know it all. I couldn't really see what her problem was, the route had been shut off to all other traffic for safety reasons anyway.

Fortunately, after giving us her two pennies worth she left with a bunch of other people to continue with the ride. About twenty minutes later we drank up and followed suit. We cycled up a smallish hill and once at the top saw absolute carnage in front of us. Eight or nine cyclists had somehow run into each other and there were bikes and bodies everywhere. I don't know if it was recognised as an accident black spot or not, but the St John's Ambulance people were already on the scene sorting people out with their cuts and bruises. They seemed to have everything under their control, so we just slowed down to pass them safely and continued with our ride.

I couldn't help but notice that one of the cyclists that had been knocked over was the girl that had been lecturing us twenty minutes earlier at the pub. As I passed her, I caught her attention and said 'it's a bloody good job we stayed for another beer, that could have been me that had been knocked off my bike'

We later learned that nobody was seriously hurt and that everyone that had been involved in the accident had managed to carry on and complete the ride in full. As for us lot, we had several celebratory drinks on the seafront in Brighton and then headed back to my brother's house to off load the bikes and get down to some serious drinking and a BBQ.

I stayed at my brothers for the night and drove home the following day around lunchtime.

Venice

My missus decided that she wanted to end our relationship and left me when the kids were about fifteen and thirteen years old to move into a rented place in Broadstairs. I stayed in the house thinking at first that she would move back home as soon as she came to her senses. It wasn't long before I realized that this was not to be the case, so I contacted a local estate agent's office to put the house up for sale.

Rowanne had moved with her mother to Broadstairs and Lauren had opted to stay with me at the house. Both of the kids were able to stay with either of us as both houses had plenty of bedrooms.

I hated being on my own and it wasn't long before I became very friendly with one of my sister's mates Cath. I had known her for years but had never envisaged that I would end up sleeping with her. She stayed over a couple of times when neither of the kids were home and I suggested to her that we could bugger off for the weekend on holiday.

I searched through the internet and found some cheap tickets with Ryanair to fly to Venice. It wasn't a situation where we were madly in love, it was more the fact that we were good friends with a few benefits thrown in. She needed a holiday, and I needed the company, so we booked it up on the understanding that there were no strings attached. It was pure coincidence, but it turned out that we were going away to Venice on the 13th of February and would be there for Valentine's day.

I didn't really know what to say to Rowanne and Lauren about it, they had had more than enough to deal with as it was. I thought that the last thing they would want to know was that their dad was going on holiday with another bird, so I decided to use the story they were familiar with. I told them that they would have to stay with their mother for the weekend because I was going away with a bunch of coppers for a charity bike ride in Venice.

Everything went according to plan, the kids went to the house in Broadstairs without any problems, I picked Cath up from her place and off we went to the airport to catch our flight. As far as anyone other than my sister was concerned, I was off on a bike ride to Venice with the usual crowd of cyclists.

On arrival in Venice, we managed to locate a hotel without too much of a problem. We paid for a couple of nights and then we dropped our bags in our room and went to see what the place had to offer. I was gob smacked, I had told everyone that I was going away on a bike ride and there were no roads to cycle on. It had never entered my head that Venice was famous for its canals, its waterways and its Gondola's. In the whole time we were there we never saw a single car.

We had a great weekend, we did plenty of 'people watching' whilst sat in the bars, we ate well, and we did some of the culture stuff as well. Three days wasn't long enough to see it all, but it was a good laugh while it lasted.

Before we knew it. the weekend was over, and we were boarding the plane again to return home. I didn't say anything to Cath, but I was wondering to myself how long it would be before the cat was out of the bag and Debi found out what had really gone on. Not that it should have mattered, she was the one that had called everything off in the first place.

Sure enough, it wasn't very long before I had my ex on the phone. 'You haven't been on a bike ride at all have you, she screamed, 'you have been to Venice for the weekend with that fucking Cath haven't you'. Before I could reply she went on to say, 'there's no chance of me ever coming home now is there, not after this'.

It was unbelievable, she was the one that had walked out of our relationship, and now, as if by some sort of a miracle it was my fault that we had split up. I waited for her to calm down and casually said, 'you had no intention of coming home any time soon, so I have moved on with my life' and then I hung up.

And Finally

I could go on with this book forever, I have still got loads of stories and the best part of twenty years to go that I haven't even mentioned at all. Unfortunately, I have found myself in a situation where I have not really got any choice other than to cut the book short. My main aim was always to be able to give a copy of this book to my parents and each of my kids. The thought of selling hundreds of copies and making loads of money never ever came into the equation, although it would obviously be the icing on the cake if it did prove to be popular and I sold a few.

As things stand, my poor old dad is suffering with his health. He is in his eighties and has gone downhill over the last few years. He may only have a few months to go, he may have years, it's one of those situations. One thing is for sure, and that is the simple fact that the clock is ticking. It is my intention to get this book to him while I still have the chance and the nicest thing that could happen to me is if he were to turn around to me four or five years from now and say something like, 'You should have known that you had plenty of time to finish your book, I wasn't ready to go then and I'm still not ready.' Possibly, if I find myself in this situation, I will be able to say something back to him like 'I am pleased about that because here is part two'.

18586552R00109

Printed in Great Britain
by Amazon